MUMBAI'S MOST WANTED

MUMBAI'S MOST WANTED

THE THRILLING CASEFILES OF A SUPERCOP

MADHUKAR ZENDE

WITH

JAI VIJAYA MADHUKAR ZENDE

HARPER
NON-FICTION

First published in India by Harper Non-Fiction 2025
An imprint of HarperCollins *Publishers* India
HarperCollins *Publishers* India, Cyber City, Building 10-A, Gurugram,
Haryana – 122002, India
www.harpercollins.co.in

2 4 6 8 10 9 7 5 3 1

P-ISBN: 978-93-6569-124-5
E-ISBN: 978-93-6569-841-1

Typeset in 11.5/15 Scala Sans Pro
by HarperCollins *Publishers* India Pvt. Ltd

Printed and bound at
Replika Press Pvt. Ltd.

MIX
Paper | Supporting responsible forestry
FSC™ C016779

This book is produced from independently certified FSC® paper to ensure responsible forest management.

HarperCollins *Publishers*, Macken House, 39/40 Mayor Street Upper,
Dublin 1, D01 C9W8, Ireland

DISCLAIMER

This book is inspired by real events and historical occurrences. While the factual elements present the Author's experiences as a police officer as accurately as possible, some of the dialogue between characters comprises fictionalized conversations, which are intended to reflect the likely tone, emotions and interactions of the individuals involved, and to enhance the storytelling. They should not be taken as direct quotations or verbatim records of any actual discussions. Any resemblance to actual spoken words or private exchanges is coincidental, and liberties have been taken for the purpose of facilitating narrative clarity and flow.

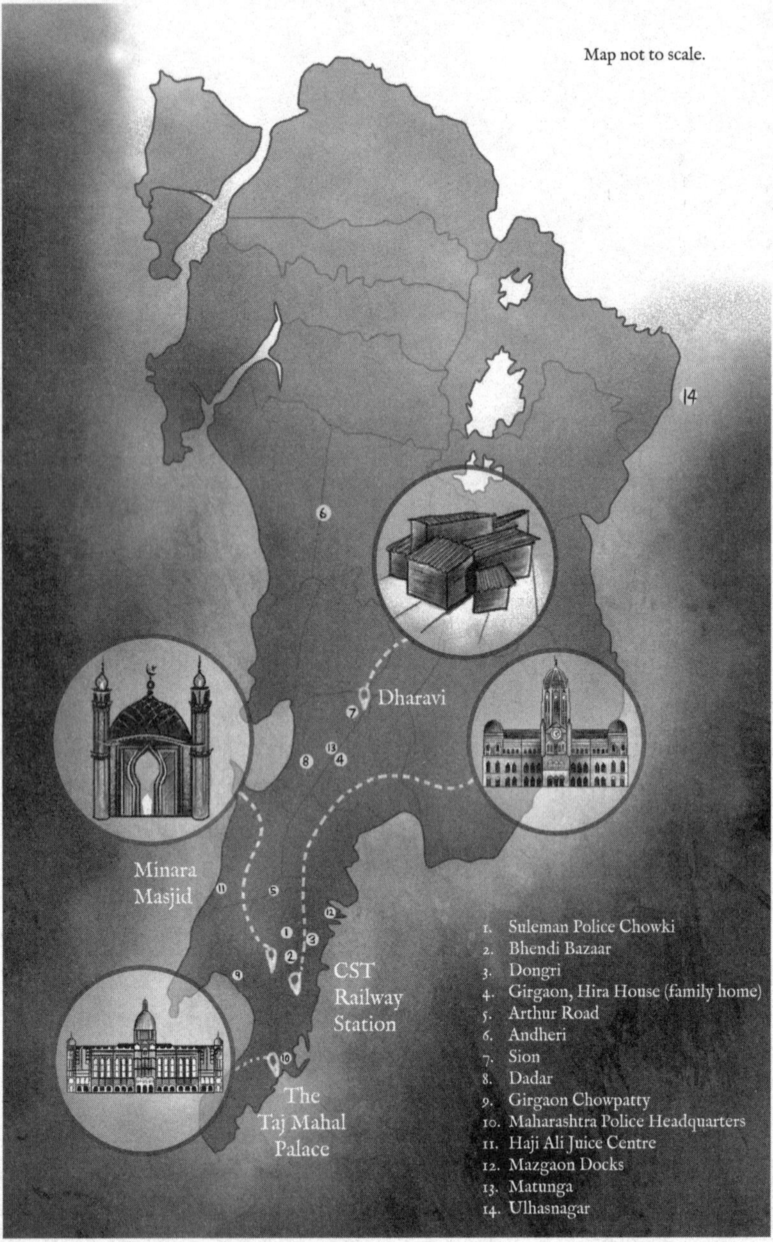
Map not to scale.
14
6
Dharavi
7
13
8
4
Minara
Masjid
11
5
12
1
3
2
CST
Railway
Station
9
10
The
Taj Mahal
Palace
1. Suleman Police Chowki
2. Bhendi Bazaar
3. Dongri
4. Girgaon, Hira House (family home)
5. Arthur Road
6. Andheri
7. Sion
8. Dadar
9. Girgaon Chowpatty
10. Maharashtra Police Headquarters
11. Haji Ali Juice Centre
12. Mazgaon Docks
13. Matunga
14. Ulhasnagar

To
the Mumbai Police

CONTENTS

Foreword by S. Hussain Zaidi xi

Introduction: The Making of a Police Officer xvii

1. Murder on the Mumbai Local 1
2. The Deadly Riots of Pydhonie 32
3. The Rise and Arrest of Charles Sobhraj 56
4. The Sensational Fall of the Serpent 80
5. *Shakti*'s Producer Is Kidnapped! 116
6. The Brutal Murder of Babu Reshim 139
7. Underworld Menace: Mastan to Dawood 170
8. Dharavi: The Incredible Transformation of Asia's Largest Slum 200

Acknowledgements 223

FOREWORD

Zindadil Zende

Since his retirement as assistant commissioner of police (ACP) in 1996, fate has afforded me several opportunities to cross paths with Madhukar Zende—a man whose legacy in the Mumbai Police force is as enduring as it is inspiring. When I met him again in 2012 at the launch of my book in Mumbai, I was struck by the enduring sharpness of his mind. Even at seventy-four, he could effortlessly pinpoint factual discrepancies in my work, a testament to a wisdom and attention to detail that has only deepened with time.

A Storied Career and an Unassuming Demeanour

Madhukar Zende—affectionately known as Zende Saab—is not just a name, but a symbol of unwavering commitment to justice and a beacon of integrity within the Mumbai Police. His illustrious career, spanning several decades, is punctuated not only by high-profile cases but by a relentless pursuit of truth and fairness. Zende Saab's razor-sharp memory and encyclopedic knowledge of the force's history and operations have long set him apart. In an environment where accolades can sometimes inflate egos, he remains refreshingly humble—a true paradox of extraordinary professional achievement paired with genuine modesty.

Moments of Unyielding Courage

Throughout his career, Zende demonstrated a fearless resolve that became the stuff of legend. In 1964, when the notorious smuggler Haji Mastan assaulted a police constable, it was Zende who took the bold step of arresting him—a move that would stand as Mastan's only conviction until his later arrest during the Emergency in 1977. This single, defining act of defiance against a powerful criminal not only underscored his commitment to duty but also set a precedent for the force.

In another riveting episode, the courage of Zende Saab shone through when two constables were ambushed by five knife-wielding robbers. With a fearsome roar and a determination that left little room for hesitation, he charged into the melee—unarmed yet undeterred—single-handedly subduing the attackers. Such incidents reveal a man who was always prepared to risk everything in the service of law and order, epitomizing the spirit of a true guardian of justice.

A Mastermind of Investigative Policing

Yet, Zende's legacy is not solely built on acts of physical bravery. His methodical and relentless investigative prowess has been equally instrumental in his storied career. His tireless pursuit of justice led to the capture of the elusive Charles Sobhraj—dubbed the 'Bikini Killer'—not once, but on two separate occasions. In 1971, through a blend of strategic planning and unyielding perseverance, he secured Sobhraj's first arrest. Later, in 1986, an audacious operation executed in a south Mumbai restaurant resulted in the criminal's second capture. These landmark arrests not only testify to his tactical brilliance but also underscore his dedication to dismantling criminal networks that jeopardized public safety.

Leadership in Times of Crisis

Zende's leadership was further tested during the turbulent riots of 1992–93. Serving as the ACP of the Pydhonie Division at the time, he emerged as a steadying force amid chaos. His ability to maintain order and safeguard the local populace during one of Mumbai's most volatile periods is a testament to his exceptional crisis management skills and empathetic approach to policing. His calm demeanour and strategic acumen during such crises have left an indelible mark on the collective memory of the community.

An Enduring Legacy

Madhukar Zende's contributions to law enforcement transcend the mere tally of arrests or accolades. His career is a rich tapestry woven from threads of courage, meticulous investigation and an unwavering commitment to justice. Zende Saab's life vividly illustrates how a steadfast adherence to duty—when paired with humility and integrity—can transform adversity into triumph and challenges into enduring milestones.

Every interaction with him has been a lesson in character. His very presence radiates a spirit that continues to inspire not only his contemporaries but also future generations of law enforcement officers. His name alone spelled doom for numerous career criminals during his tenure at the crime branch—a rare honour reserved for those who command genuine respect and instil fear in the hearts of wrongdoers.

Despite his towering accomplishments, Zende Saab has always shunned the limelight. His modesty and reluctance to court publicity stand in stark contrast to the conventional image of a celebrated officer. Yet, it was precisely these qualities—his courage, unwavering conviction and deep-seated integrity—that drew journalists and the public alike to the flame of a truly admirable man of character.

When I once inquired about the secret behind his extraordinary success, his response was simple and profound: 'Zindagi Zindadili ka naam hain ...' In those few words lay the essence of his philosophy—a life defined by fearless vitality, an indomitable spirit that refused to be subdued by the challenges of duty.

As you turn the pages of this book, you will encounter not just one, but scores of incidents that vividly capture his 'zindadili'—a spirit that remains as relevant and inspiring today as it was during the days of his active service. Madhukar Zende's legacy, a blend of fearless action, astute investigation and humble leadership, continues to light the path for all who dare to serve with honour and integrity.

S. Hussain Zaidi

INTRODUCTION: THE MAKING OF A POLICE OFFICER

On 2 July 1960, I was on top of the world. I had joined the Esplanade police station as a sub-inspector, fulfilling my greatest ambition. Just over a year earlier, on 13 May 1959, I had married Vijaya, the prettiest girl in my neighbourhood in Nana Peth, Pune, and the love of my life since I was fourteen. Sometimes, it baffles me how all the pieces had aligned so beautifully to form a complete picture.

I had always dreamed of being a police officer. My greatest inspiration was my grandfather, Vitthal Zende. He was one of the founding members of the Shivaji Maratha School in Pune. Although not a rich man, he played an important role in erecting the very first major public statue of Chhatrapati Shivaji Maharaj in 1928. His leadership even compelled the Scindia Maharaja of

Gwalior to make a hefty donation towards erecting this statue. Prominent freedom fighters like Keshavrao Jedhe were regular visitors to our home in Pune.

My cousin, Babasaheb Adhav, eight years my senior and a medical doctor with a strong socialist bent, got involved with the Samyukta Maharashtra movement (a public movement in the 1950s to include Mumbai in Maharashtra). Through him, I was exposed to the ideologies of leaders like S.M. Joshi and Bhai Vaidya, who were fountains of rationalist and socialist thought. Babasaheb Adhav played an instrumental role in anti-caste movements like '*ek gav ek panavtha*' ('one well for one village', as a means to end discrimination) and Satyashodhak Samaj (truth-seekers' society, which fought against superstitions).

My own parents, Bapurao and Sindhutai, did their utmost to support their less-fortunate siblings and neighbours, even at great cost to themselves. Two widowed sisters, and their children, had come back to their paternal home after their husbands' deaths, and my parents welcomed them.

I grew up in a brood of twenty-three siblings and cousins. Thanks to the web of relationships in this large household, I learnt to call my parents Tai (older sister) and Mama (maternal uncle), probably because that's what my Atyas (father's sisters) and my older cousins would call them. We had close ties with our neighbours in Pune and in Zendewadi, our ancestral village, where we spent large parts of the year. We had some custard apple and fig trees in the village. The figs of that region, Purandar, now even have a GI tag. There were seasonal harvests of local mangoes (including one that tasted like dill). Some siblings or neighbours' kids and I would routinely ferry sacks or baskets of the season's farm produce on foot, or on a bullock-cart or bus to the nearby Saswad market. Many of the neighbours were part of the extended family, and we maintained close ties and looked out for each other. Even now, people in Zendewadi call me Dada (older brother). We learnt that compassion, courage, hard work and integrity were the signs of an evolved person, not money and social position.

Why I Became a Cop

During my teens, I had been a member of the Rashtra Seva Dal. This was a voluntary organization that was nurtured by the Indian National Congress to foster a sense of duty towards the nation. We learnt martial exercises and dances, volunteered in the local community and read about nation-builders from across the globe. We also listened to stories, such as Shivaji Maharaj's lifelong struggle to free Maharashtra from Mughal rule, Abraham Lincoln's leadership in freeing African-Americans from slavery and how India's first general (later field marshal) K.M. Cariappa led our army post-Independence. These stories taught me that no oppressor is so strong that they cannot be fought against.

Through all these experiences, I developed an aspiration to serve India and its people. I decided to join the Indian Army.

I was not very good at studies and had failed my Intermediate examination after Grade 11 on the first attempt. This put paid to my aspirations to join the army that year. I did not have the luxury of time—my father was out of work, and I needed to start earning soon. I decided to appear for the police sub-inspector recruitment examinations for Maharashtra state. I did well in the exams and was selected for the physical. Luckily, I was a good runner and an all-round strong sportsman. I was also an active member of the National Cadet Corps. These helped me pass the police selection procedures with flying colours in 1959. Passing the Intermediate examination was a requirement to become a sub-inspector, and eventually, I did that too.

I emerged as the best outdoor cadet in my batch, and on 1 May 1960, on the occasion of the inauguration of the state of Maharashtra, I was asked to command a platoon of the Maharashtra Police marching squad. It was a rare honour for a not-yet sub-inspector, and a great start to a very fulfilling thirty-seven years for me in the Maharashtra Police.

The Qualities of a Good Policeman

Over the course of my career as a policeman, I received a lot of love and respect from the citizens and my teams, as well as guidance and inspiration from senior officers and other great people who I interacted with. I won some rare accolades, including being the first officer to win a President's Police Medal for Distinguished Service and a Police Medal for Meritorious Service in successive years, and received a fair bit of fame. There is a pretty good chance that that is why you are reading this book. Some of the cases and incidents I worked on became quite famous, and people often ask me to recount those experiences. This book gives you an in-depth look into seven of them.

But before we get into them, I want to talk about a question that has been on my mind these days. There are nearly two lakh policemen in Maharashtra, and about twenty lakh across India. I think all good policemen exhibit a common set of qualities and behaviours. Quite likely, these qualities apply to any field of work—whether you are a professional in the corporate space, an entrepreneur or even someone who simply wants to lead a life with purpose and grace.

Early in my career, there were a few incidents where these qualities came to the fore, and were life-changing for me. These incidents taught me lessons that were formative as a policeman, a leader of people, and as a human being. I would like to share these incidents with you. Perhaps, they will help you in your own journeys.

A Genuine Desire to Serve People

The police are a service, not a force. The service exists *for* the people, and is supported everyday *by* the people.

A police personnel cannot take this support for granted. They must earn the support and trust of the people with their actions and by engaging with the people and their lives.

A policeman is a very social creature. Working with people, for them, and making a direct impact on their lives is the most satisfying aspect of a policeman's life. Seeing a policeman engage with the community this way nurtures trust about the police in the minds of the citizenry. They support police work and maintain peace and order in their own communities. This police–public partnership is the leverage that makes it possible for a few thousand policemen to maintain peace in cities of tens of millions. Here's a story that illustrates this idea.

In Mumbai, before cricket became the one sport to rule them all, football was very popular. In the 1970s, Rovers Cup was one of India's premier football tournaments. Clubs from all over India participated. And since Mumbai (known as Bombay then) had working populations from all over the country, each club had deep and passionate backing. The Goans supported Dempo and Salgaocar; the Bengalis thronged for Mohun Bagan and East Bengal, the Muslims among them had extra love for Mohammedan Sporting. Mumbai's textile mills like Mafatlal and Orkay had their own teams. Each of these communities were very vocal about football, and after a few drinks, the passion would boil over into verbal and physical volleys against the opponents of the day. Quarrels and fisticuffs were commonplace. The

Cooperage Football Ground near Nariman Point, now the home of some Mumbai Football League clubs, was the home of Rovers Cup. The 30,000-seater stadium in the heart of Mumbai was always packed to the rafters, and there would be long queues to enter well before the matches started. Stragglers, hawkers, ticket-scalpers and other opportunists added to the numbers and the general melee. Naturally, we deployed a good number of lathi-wielding policemen to maintain relative calm. And since prevention is better than cure, I would strike up conversations among the fans, engage in friendly banter and break up petty squabbles. This served the dual purpose of helping me get a sense of which match was likely to get more heated based on the pre-match debates, and also made me a familiar figure among the regulars, the most passionate fans.

In 1977, Tata Sports Club and Dempo were playing the semi-final of the Rovers Cup. The stadium was packed; the game was in full swing. In the twelfth minute, Tata had possession. The ball was passed into the penalty area, and their forward slipped it in. A goal in the first fifteen minutes. Ten thousand people erupted in celebration. Another ten thousand let out shocked gasps. But then, the referee signalled off-side and disallowed the goal. The celebration and gasps were reversed in the stadium. The Tata team would have none of this. They were not going to be denied the goal. When the referee refused to back down, they walked off the field. Obviously, there were no video replays back then which could've helped.

There was stunned silence for a minute or two in the stadium. Then it hit the fans—if the team had walked off, the game would be cancelled, and they would not get their hard-earned money's worth. This was not okay. Slowly, chants of '*Paisa vaapas do! Paisa vaapas do!* (Give back our money!)' erupted. Fans of both sides joined in this demand.

A man called Mr Ziauddin was in charge of the Cooperage Ground. He would have none of this, and flatly refused to return any money. The fans' frustration then literally went up in flames as one fan broke his wooden-plank seat and set it on fire. Others took the cue, and slowly, a large part of the stadium was ablaze. If you remember the sights broadcast around the world from the India–Sri Lanka semi-final of the 1996 Cricket World Cup at Kolkata's Eden Gardens, this was pretty similar to that. If this continued, not only would the stadium burn down, but Mumbai's decades-old football tradition would be in danger.

Ziauddin was shocked and started panicking. He tried to shout the people down, but nothing worked. I had to do something. I told him, 'You must promise that if I stop this arson and save your stadium, you must give refunds.' Before he could affirm, I snatched a blackboard used for keeping scores, and wrote in large letters, 'PUT OUT THE FIRE. WE WILL REFUND.'

I held the board above my head and started walking around the ground, also shouting out the message in my loudest voice. I had no reason to think anyone would believe me, a policeman, regarding refunds. It was the passions of 30,000 people against one man trying to restore calm. But I had to try. My naturally booming voice was barely audible even to myself. My throat was going dry, and it hurt from shouting, as did my arms from carrying the big board. Sweat streamed down my body in the heat of the evening. But slowly, one fire went out, then another, and another. People wanted to believe me, and they did. They loved their game, and the stadium. No one wanted it to end this way, and I was giving them a way out. Being a familiar and trusted face helped them to believe me.

The stadium was saved. Ziauddin offered the option of an on-the-spot refund or using the same tickets the next day for a replay of the match. A few hundred took the refund, but most opted to come back.

The next evening, the stadium seemed to be even more packed than usual. As soon as I entered the ground with the other policemen, there was a cheer from a section of the crowd. Then others joined in. There were chants of 'Zende zindabad! Zende zindabad! (long live, Zende!)'. It was overwhelming. I had to do a lap of the stadium waving to the crowd, acknowledging their cheers like a winning team's captain. My heart was filled to bursting. I knew then that this support of the people, and the opportunity to help them, was my biggest motivator as a policeman. That evening for me was far more memorable than any other moment in my career.

Stepping into the Leader's Shoes Unprompted

Designations and titles do not make a leader. Leadership comes from a burning desire to make a change, and the passion to run towards the fire. This is how I first learnt it.

After graduating from the Police Training School, my first posting was in Mumbai. When I moved there in June 1960, I had nowhere to live. So, I left my belongings in the cloakroom of the Victoria Terminus (now Chhatrapati Shivaji Maharaj Terminus) railway station and reported to work at the Esplanade police station (now Azad Maidan police station).

For the first five days, I made some sleeping arrangements at a police officers' resthouse on Princess Street (now Shamaldas Gandhi Marg). We slept there on wooden beds without any mattresses or sheets, and used the public facilities down the road for our morning ablutions. Then, the kind Inspector Pesi Doctor allowed me and another freshly recruited sub-inspector to stay in his servants' room. This was above the Esplanade police station. We rented a bed each for three rupees a month, and since the room did not have a toilet or bathroom, we would bathe at an open-air public tap on Picket Road. Since I did not have a home, Vijaya was still staying with her father in Pune (and he charged her a monthly rent). She visited me every month. Since I sent almost my entire salary to my parents in Pune, she would save a few rupees from her monthly salary of Rs 200 and secretly leave them in the pockets of my uniform. I worked almost all the time, and even volunteered to do the work of others in the police station. So, I learnt rapidly and became popular among my colleagues too. Life was good.

The Esplanade/Azad Maidan police station was built in the days of British rule. It included a fairly large prison cell of about 300 square feet, including toilet space. Since it was quite spacious, other law-enforcement branches like the Customs, Pathan Branch (it dealt chiefly with issues pertaining to the substantial Pathan community in the city), Anti-Gambling Squad, etc. also locked up their prisoners who were pending trial there. The cell would sometimes accommodate almost a hundred prisoners. They slept on beds that were basically fat wooden planks, or on the floor. Toilets were holes in the ground. But that was the state of prison cells everywhere, and no one paid much heed to improving them.

One afternoon, I was doing some paperwork in the police station. It was a hot day, and the few fans installed there were not very effective. There were no fans in the cell. On this dour, still day, there were some very loud bangs heard from the direction of the cell. Everyone ran to see what had happened. A small riot was starting to rumble.

Something had angered the cellmates to the point where they grabbed the planks that were their beds and broke them to make rough wooden weapons. Some others grabbed faeces from the toilets. They challenged policemen to fight them. They announced their intentions to force open the cell lock and run away. Many of them were muscled street fighters, and they could certainly have made a legitimate attempt to run away. It would have been a terrible disgrace and would have led to so many criminals suddenly being let loose.

A deputy inspector on duty at the police station was the first to run away. Many other policemen also ran or hid. Worse, some were ready to free the violent mob, rather than try to contain them in their cell. At least that would save the lives of the policemen in the station, they said. As a new officer, who felt immensely proud to be wearing the uniform, such capitulation was out of the question. There was no question of flight. I was going to fight. But how?

I trusted my gut. The service rifles belonging to the armoury of the police station stood on a wooden rack a few feet from me. I knew they were not loaded, but the prisoners did not. I seized that advantage, picked up one gun, and rushed towards the cell, facing the rioting mob.

'Let's shoot these bastards! They want to run, and they think they can scare us. Let's show them what a Bombay policeman can do to them. Let's shoot all those who want to fight us. I will shoot the first one who tries to hit me or to run away. Come on! Who wants to be shot first?' I challenged them.

The prisoners and goons were stunned and froze in their tracks. This inspired a few other cops in the station, and they joined me—with or without guns.

Very quickly the rioting prisoners started to back down. At first, there remained a few boisterous ones. But eventually, all of the rioters retreated and dropped their weapons. We moved the particularly aggressive ones into different cells.

This was my first lesson in crowd control. When you stand up to a rioting mob and plant doubt in their minds, their will breaks, and you seize the advantage.

This logic came in handy many times. In the 1960s and 1970s, there were a lot of morchas (protest marches) in Bombay. Many of them culminated in stone-throwing, breaking of public property like streetlights, buses, taxis, and even private cars parked on the roads. Many mobs would also target the poorly armed and lightly protected policemen that would try to stop them. I learnt that if we stopped three or four of the lead perpetrators, it would break the will of the mob, and they would stop their violence. The bigger lesson of the incident with the rioting prisoners was about leadership.

Be Proud of the Work You Do

Being a policeman was not just a job from 10 a.m. to 6 p.m., nor was it restricted to the jurisdiction that I was posted in. If I could help as a policeman, or indeed as a person, I would always step in. Personal safety, place and cost just did not matter. This attitude has always made a difference in my life, and it still does.

The annual ten-day Ganpati festival is my favourite time of the year. Having grown up in pre-Independence Pune, the sarvajanik (public) Ganpati celebrations and immersion processions were a big part of my life. Each year, I danced in the lezim pathaks (squads of dancers of the folk form of lezim). These are groups of twenty or more young boys who dance in formation to a heavy percussion beat played on a drum that travels with them. They can still be seen each year during the Ganpati immersion processions in Pune. I used to put my heart and soul into these dances.

In 1970, I was transferred to Gamdevi police station as a sub-inspector. I was very excited that I could now witness the even larger Ganpati processions of Mumbai at close quarters. Thousands walked and danced in these processions and converged on Girgaon Chowpatty. The processions ran well past midnight. Thanks to the beautiful Arabian Sea shoreline, even ten- and fifteen-feet-tall Ganpati idols could be immersed by going deeper into the waters.

But there was one problem. Each year, as people waded into the water, some of them would get lost at sea. Their cries for help would go unheeded. There would be absolutely no lighting at Chowpatty. So, no one could see where the cries of help would come from. Also, as thousands thronged the beach, with no crowd control there were instances of people being trampled upon. Miscreants would take advantage of the dark, and there would be a lot of untoward incidents.

It really pained my heart to see this beautiful celebration marred by such events. I figured a simple solution like installing a few floodlights on the beach would go a long way in solving this problem.

This was not a solution that the Mumbai Police could execute; it needed BEST (Bombay Electric Supply and Transport, as it was then called). In my ten years as a Mumbai Police officer, I had learnt that in this city, all departments are keen to help the citizens. Sometimes bureaucracy gets in the way, but if someone is willing to take the initiative and navigate, major problems can be solved.

I approached the chief engineer of BEST, Mr Mhatre. He needed the approval of the municipal commissioner, M.W. Desai—one of the most competent men in the city, with a strong bias for action. Luckily, I had worked closely with Desai once before, to construct a one-acre sized dance floor (don't ask). When I approached him, he immediately called Mhatre and got the required work order issued. Within a few weeks, four high-powered halogen lights were installed on Chowpatty. It became a much safer place for Ganpati celebrations, and a safer place all-around.

It was a great first-hand experience to work with all the guardians and caretakers of the city, and make my own small contribution to the most beloved celebrations in Mumbai and Maharashtra. Morya!

Be Nimble and Open to Improvising

No two days are the same for a policeman, as we are called in only in extraordinary situations. A policeman must be able to improvise on the spot based on the specific situation. To improvise effectively, it is vital to be sensitive to the situation and the feelings of the people involved. It is equally vital to have in-depth knowledge of the laws—the letter of the law, its relevance and its spirit. Only then can a policeman apply those well and suggest changes when appropriate.

I joined the police service expecting to protect the people from criminals and other miscreants. One afternoon in the winter of 1963, I was amusingly disabused of this notion.

I was on jury duty at the sessions court near Kala Ghoda. My job was to chaperone the jury at the court (juries were phased out of Indian law a decade later), which meant making sure they observed the rules, like staying put in the chamber, not meeting anyone outside the permitted group, etc. There was an hour's lunch break from 12.30 p.m. to 1.30 p.m.; just enough time to take a bus to the G.T. Hospital doctors' canteen for a meal that cost twelve annas (seventy-five paise), and another fifteen-minute bus ride back to the court.

That day, I was riding shotgun on a single-decker BEST bus—a small perk for a uniformed policeman. I was enjoying the breeze blowing in my face. As the bus neared Khadi Gramodyog, near Flora Fountain, I noticed some panic among the pedestrians. They were running helter-skelter shouting, '*Hatti! Hatti!*'

Bemused by the situation and the accompanying shouts, I jumped off the moving bus, narrowly avoiding the cars that also seemed to be veering and criss-crossing. I turned around and saw an actual, live elephant running on the busiest thoroughfare in India's financial capital. It was a magical sight, and were it not for the people running in fear for their lives, it would have been very funny. The elephant too was probably panicking at the sight of these people, and the noise of the traffic, and running aimlessly but quite fast—considering it was an elephant in a metropolis.

My natural policing instincts kicked in. I had to get the elephant to a less crowded area. Perhaps, there was a way. There was a renowned sugarcane juice seller right there, who had big bundles of sugarcane lying on the footpath. Elephants love sugarcane, so that was to be the bait. In those days, there were a lot of manual labourers in Mumbai who carried heavy loads on hand-pulled carts. Flora Fountain, being close to the trading area, always had a few handcarts standing by the side of the road. I had a plan.

I grabbed a bundle of sugarcane and waved it in the direction of the elephant. Once I had its attention, it started running towards me. I had a panicked elephant charging right at me. Perfect!

I flung the sugarcane onto a nearby handcart and started pulling it. The elephant was bearing down on it. Somehow, I ran faster than an elephant chasing his favourite food.

The roads parallel to D.N. Road along the docks were generally less crowded, so I ran in that direction. People were now feeling safer, so the pedestrians and cars moved aside to let me pass. Some of them even stopped to cheer me on, though a bit cautiously, so they would not scare the elephant too much. I ran, looking around for a place where the elephant could be sequestered and allowed to enjoy his meal in peace.

After about ten minutes, I noticed the black iron gate of the Customs Warehouse. It was open and showed a large gravelly yard. Luckily, it was empty. That place could be reasonably expected to be nearly deserted at this hour. I was getting exhausted pulling this massive load, but the adrenaline kept me going. I dragged the cart deep into the Customs Warehouse yard, and the elephant duly followed. Before it reached the cart, I dropped the handles I was holding, spun around and ran a safe distance back towards the gate. The elephant got to his snack and dug in.

Relieved, I ran out of the gate, and with another effort of will, pulled it shut. Film aficionados may understand when I say I felt like Amitabh Bachchan from *Deewar* coming out of the warehouse after beating Peter, even though that film was released over a decade after this event.

A small crowd was applauding me outside. I sauntered over to a nearby sugarcane juice seller, and enjoyed a full glass with ice and a squeeze of lemon, or as we call it locally, '*nimbu maarke*'.

The area I had led the elephant through is home to many newspaper offices, and most of them picked up the story of the policeman who arrested the elephant after a chase in the heart of Mumbai. My name was in the papers the next day, as a 'tale of valour'. Seniors and colleagues everywhere reached out to congratulate me. I was feted everywhere as the '*jigarbaaz porya*' (brave young cop) in town. I loved it!

Policing Is Only Half the Job of Law-Enforcement

An important manifestation of knowing the law is to be able to prosecute a case well. All the energy, resources and effort put into the detective work and arresting a suspect are wasted if the case is not prosecuted well. The actual prosecution depends on the lawyers, but a policeman must work closely with them. A policeman's job is only complete when the criminal receives the punishment laid down by law.

As mentioned before, Vijaya and I were living in different cities. We kept up our commuting relationship for about two years while I moved between temporary bachelor pads. Late in 1962, we were expecting our first child, and my request for a government quarter was granted. We moved into a one-bedroom flat in the Dena Bank building, Third Pasta Lane, Colaba. It was a nice part of town, not far from the docks and fishing villages. I kept up a hectic work schedule, and time permitting, we enjoyed trying out the street food. Rose falooda was one of our all-time favourites.

One evening, my six-month-pregnant wife and I were sharing a fruit juice near Sassoon Docks, following a short stroll. This daily routine was the little bit of 'us' time that we got. In those days, evening traffic was minimal, and even the streetlights were not very bright. There were a few stragglers and homeless men around. Overall, the streets felt calm, although not necessarily very safe. Not all the men walking around had clean intentions. As an officer who worked in the area, some of them were familiar to me.

Sada Mahadik was a local tough guy. He strolled up to the juice seller we were standing at, and calmly demanded a juice. He picked up a glass, as if inspecting its cleanliness.

'No, first clear your past dues,' the seller replied in a small, quaking voice.

'Aye, how dare you ask me for money? Be happy I am letting you operate here!' Sada threatened, dropping the glass on the footpath, stepping on it and crushing a shard.

The crunching sound grated on my ears, even though I tried to keep calm.

'Sada, please don't do this. I am a poor juice seller ...'

Sada picked up one more glass and dropped it.

I could not help but step in.

'Sada, you heard him. Pay him or walk away,' I spoke calmly.

'Saalya! Who are you to butt in?' Sada turned his attention to me, glass in hand.

'I am a police officer.'

'Achha?' asked Sada, and broke the third glass on my head.

My head swam and my ears rang. I thought I would faint. Blood was streaming down my face. Vijaya had never seen blood before. And here we were, an expecting couple on a quiet evening walk, with blood streaming down my face, and God knew what was going to come next. She started to shiver in panic.

The sensible thing would have been to back off from this confrontation and walk home with her. But there was no way was I going to do that. This goon needed to be taught a lesson, and I would do it.

I grabbed his collar. But before I could get a good grip, he got free and made a run for it. He ran into a building across the street.

I reassured my wife that everything would be fine, and she should walk home. I would be back in some time. She had faith in me. She squeezed my hand, whispered, 'Come soon!', and slowly made her way home.

I ran towards the building after Sada. Luckily, for me, my dear friend and Police Training School batchmate, Shyam Kundalkar, was strolling nearby. I hurriedly explained the situation to him, and we both ran up the narrow stairs of the building.

It was a short chase. Sada was on the third-floor terrace of that building, hiding behind the water tank. We pulled him out and dragged him to the local police station. He got some police treatment first before being put away in the cell.

When the case came up for hearing, naturally, the juice seller was a key witness. But he now claimed to not recall the events of the evening. This upset the judge immensely.

'What sort of prosecution is this? Do you not have one decent witness?' he reprimanded us.

Luckily, the case was watertight even without the juice seller's testimony. Sada was sentenced to six months in prison.

I learnt a valuable lesson that day—that policing is only half the job of law-enforcement. If we didn't prosecute properly with a watertight case in alignment with the Code of Criminal Procedure, and other laws and processes of the country, then even the most dreaded criminal can easily walk free.

Do the Right Thing, Follow the Voice in Your Heart

The final quality of good policing I want to talk about is the conviction to do the right thing. This can go beyond the limitations of what the law, or senior officers, or indeed anyone else has to say. Your inner voice must be the final guide. To hone this, it is very important to understand the wider social context; to read and be informed of the goings-on in the world, and to listen to and interact with people from different spheres of life.

People share their learnings and thoughts openly, but it's important to listen sensitively.

In 1964, I was posted at Paltan Road (now known as Mata Ramabai Ambedkar Road) police station. It is a beautiful heritage building dating back to 1918. Paltan refers to an army squad, and this building was constructed to house a marine battalion during colonial times.[1] Even now, there is a substantial presence of the Indian Navy in Mumbai; Navy Nagar near Colaba includes the headquarters of the Western Command, which is the navy's 'sword arm', given its location at the Arabian Sea.

Naturally, naval ships routinely dock there, and a large number of Indian Navy personnel, from seamen to a vice-admiral are based in Navy Nagar. Being a defence area, it is closed to the public and under armed protection. No civilian is permitted inside the gates without express approval. The cadets and seamen, especially those serving on ships, make their way into the city on their off days for a good time. With their strong physiques and distinctive haircuts, they are easily identifiable. Some even wear their uniform into the city as a matter of

1 Yesha Kotak, 'No history sheet on 100-year-old police stations in Mumbai', *Hindustan Times*, 10 July 2018, https://www.hindustantimes.com/mumbai-news/no-history-sheet-on-100-year-old-police-stations-in-mumbai/story-laaZgWCdss6ZEleOCdSB8N.html

pride. Like sailors on 'shore leave' everywhere, they are reputed to be a boisterous lot. But they spend well and are welcomed by the bars.

One evening, in 1965, a group of such young sailors came out from the Lion Gate in Colaba, and went to their regular haunt, a bar run by a man called James. He loved their profitable custom, but remained wary as there was only a fine line between being boisterous and starting a brawl. And if things did go badly, it would be difficult to sort out the matter. The Maharashtra Police had no jurisdiction over these defence personnel, and things could get complicated. James had recently hired a couple of new serving boys to ensure the navy-men were served quickly, in his ongoing effort to keep his customers happy. It didn't exactly work.

That day, there were about twenty navy-men being served by five servers, including the two new hires. The evening went well for a couple of hours, and James was pleased. One more round of drinks was being served, when one of the navy-men accidentally bumped into the server. A tray-full of glasses shattered to the floor, and the contents spilled on to a few of the customers. The sailors, a few drinks down, were furious, and proceeded to manhandle the server. Another server stepped in to help his colleague, and also received a couple of whacks for his team spirit. Fearing the worst, James called the cops.

A police van with a few constables reached the bar. The navy-men were laying into a couple more servers, and other bar staff. Two constables rushed forward to stop them, as they would any brawler, and got slapped in turn. Not used to such disrespect, the constables got angry, and returned the favour, slapping the sailors. This brought more of them into the fray, including some who were only strolling along. The other policemen in the van also joined in. This was now an all-out brawl between men in uniforms, white and khaki. The police were vastly outnumbered and called for reinforcements, and the brawl grew bigger.

The rival factions took up positions on either side of the road now. The navy-men were close to their Lion Gate hub, so more of them kept pouring in. They soon picked up stones and started hurling them at the police. Not being accountable to these civil law-enforcement authorities, they had no reason to hold back. The police, on the other hand, felt insulted by the disrespect to their authority, and wanted to teach these young boys a lesson. If they backed off, the local population would mock them as cowards, and that would certainly not be okay. The stage was set for a battle royale.

Although the Lion Gate area was within the jurisdiction of Colaba police station, they needed more people on the ground to handle this situation, and they requested the Paltan Road police station, where I was posted, to send a squad. I went to the spot with a squad of constables. Seeing our squad emboldened the Colaba police station team on the ground led by Sub-Inspector Jog. He ordered a lathi charge. As the policemen raced forth with their batons, the navy-men got the huge iron Lion Gate to the naval area opened. That was their territory, and the police could not come in. The armed guard at the entrance would ensure that. One of the navy-men snatched a rifle from this armed guard, shouldered it, cocked it, pointed it towards the policemen. This could have led to a disaster. If fired upon, the policemen would have had to return fire. It would have been an all-out war between two defence services of India.

I felt this had to be stopped. I rushed towards the gun-wielding navy-man and snatched it from him. I was now inside the naval base. Confused, he ran and blended into the crowd. Before I had time to run out, the huge iron panels of the Lion Gate clanged shut behind me.

Now I was confronted by scores of angry, muscled navy-men, some of them inebriated. They let me have it. I was pummelled from all sides and could do nothing but shield myself. Kicks, slaps and blows rained on my head and body. I had to somehow escape their wrath.

'Stop it! Stop it! I haven't done anything,' I kept beseeching them.

Perhaps, some of them backed off. Somehow, I was able to squeeze out of the crowd, run into the guard room and lock myself in. I lay there battered and bruised next to the closed door. My body, and especially my face, hurt like hell. I could feel a little blood inside my mouth, but there were no broken teeth, nor bones. I had no regrets for what I had done, but did wonder what would happen next. In any case, it could not happen soon enough for me.

The navy-men were pounding on the door. They told me in various Indian languages what they thought of me and other policemen, including how we probably engaged in unsavoury acts with our family members. I wanted to respond, but did so only in my own mind.

After what seemed like forever, I heard a single commanding voice. 'Boys! STOP THIS! Get back to your quarters. This is an order!'

Things gradually quietened down. As I peeked through the window, I saw a uniformed officer glaring at their retreating backs. He was flanked by some armed military policemen. He then turned around and rapped on the door to my safe haven. Gingerly, I got up, and opened the door.

Commander Om Prakash of the navy police ushered me out. The gates opened again, and we were joined by our area's deputy and assistant commissioners of police. I was handed over to them.

On the drive back, we sat in the deputy commissioner's car, with me sitting next to the driver.

'You idiot!' reprimanded the senior officer. 'Why did you snatch the rifle? Who did you think was going to save you?'

'Sorry, sir. I did not think of all that. But if we had not stopped this, it would have been very embarrassing for the country to have the police and the navy fighting each other on the streets, isn't it?' I replied in a soft but clear voice. I probably sounded all muffled through my swollen mouth.

'Hmm ...' he replied.

That evening, there was a high-level meeting between the senior officers of the Indian Navy and the Maharashtra Police. It was decided that the news of this confrontation would be completely silenced. We made sure all the media outlets got the message.

*

These experiences, and the learnings gleaned from them, stand out to me over my three decades as a cop. For most people, the life of a policeman is slightly exotic and ill-understood, mostly because not many non-policemen interact closely with us as individuals. We are hailed as heroes and celebrated as warriors on our best days, and also reviled as inept, inefficient and corrupt on the worst. We are ordinary people, who are called upon only in extraordinary situations.

Typically, policemen are only associated with detecting mysterious cases and arresting dangerous criminals. While these are certainly important, they are infrequent. Most people typically associate me with the 1986 arrest of Charles Sobhraj in Goa. But there are other, far more consequential and risk-filled incidents in my career. Lying in ambush with a team for a notorious serial killer is quite different from facing a mob of hundreds of angry rioters, or coming upon a years-old murder case in which the only clue is a pair of blood-soaked pants.

In this book, I have shared some of my most memorable experiences with you. I hope it gives you an enjoyable and informative perspective into my life as a policeman in Mumbai.

1

MURDER ON THE MUMBAI LOCAL

On Ashadhi Ekadashi (the eleventh day of the waxing moon in the Hindu month of Ashadh) every year, lakhs of 'varkaris' visit the Vithoba temple in Pandharpur, Maharashtra. For many, this is the culmination of a 250-km, twenty-one-day journey that they have undertaken on foot. This is a centuries-old tradition in Maharashtra, especially in the Saswad region where I grew up. The procession, called vari, brings the paduka (wooden slippers) of two great poet-saints of Maharashtra, Sant Dynaneshwar and Sant Tukaram, from their respective shrines in Alandi and Dehu.

The journey is a celebration of devotion. There are dhol-lezim pathaks, rhythmically dancing to the beat of manjiris (small cymbals) and chanting of 'Gyanba Tukaram'. All along the route, the varkaris are feted and welcomed into camps where the locals feed and house them. Once a varkari returns home, they are venerated; anyone who meets them touches their feet, paying respect to Vithoba himself. Many varkaris take a vow of lifelong abstinence from alcohol and non-vegetarian food. As a symbol of their vow, they wear a thin necklace of tulsi (holy basil) beads, a 'tulshimaal'.

I have walked in the vari. It is a beautiful and joyous experience, and I heartily recommend it. Over generations, my family has had many varkaris, and I have found that many of them exemplify the ethos of simple thinking and upright living.

It was one such varkari who helped solve the case of a violent murder that had been unsolved for two years.

Through the 1980s and 1990s, Mumbai was reputed to be safer than any other Indian city, especially for women. Its safe spaces made it a much better city to live and work in. It's no wonder, then, that Mumbai had lakhs of women who went to colleges across the city and did jobs of their choice. Our own two daughters, Sangita and Sharmila, benefitted from this. Sangita would travel as much as 20 km each way to college all by herself. Sharmila would work late nights at a five-star hotel and crisscrossed the city prolifically. Mumbai's reputation as a safe city went a long way in earning it the sobriquet of India's 'commercial capital'.

As the guardians of law and order in the city, the Mumbai Police and the Railway Police had the critical responsibility of upholding this safety. Through a combination of vigilant engagement in the city's civic life, swift detection and effective prosecution of crimes committed, we were a celebrated police service. Mumbaikars loved to say that their police were 'second only to London's Scotland Yard'.

It seemed a normal day in 1981, when this reputation took a big blow. A young college professor was repeatedly stabbed in the ladies' compartment of a local train in broad daylight.

Shanta Devi taught at a college in Andheri, a bustling suburb of Mumbai. As a professor of chemistry, she taught both undergraduate and graduate students. She was in her mid-thirties; a woman with a gentle manner and polite smile, she was very popular among her students.

Her husband was also a respected professor, and a community leader among teachers. Between them, they had a modest income and lived in a small flat in Sion. Community leadership and union leadership brought him in contact with some unsavoury elements. In feisty arguments with them, her husband always stood his ground. This often worried Shanta Devi.

Every morning, Shanta Devi took a Central line local train from Sion to Dadar, and then changed to the Western line to Andheri. Like most Mumbaikars, she preferred the fast trains that had fewer stops, but sometimes she had to make do with the slow ones.

On that fateful day in 1981, her lectures were scheduled for late morning. She got ready for college as usual, chose a red-and-orange chequered Venkatgiri cotton sari, and pulled its pallu firmly around her shoulders. Like so many married women, she was wearing some basic jewellery. She strapped her trusted black bag to her left shoulder, and darted out of her home around 10 a.m. She knew if she walked fast enough, she could catch the 10.14 train from Sion; and she did.

A first-class train pass was one luxury Shanta Devi allowed herself—a vegetarian, she could not stand the smell of the fisherwomen and their baskets in the second class. Also, getting a seat was easier in first class.

In fact, on that day, after she had switched trains, the first-class compartment on the Western line was completely empty. She considered entering the second-class compartment rather than travelling alone. But the clean and cushioned seats of the first class were irresistible. As the train pulled out, she exchanged a fleeting smile with the teenage girl in rags whom she saw most days at this time on the platform. This urchin was the last person to see Shanta Devi alive—other than her killers, of course.

Shanta Devi settled down, ready to enjoy some quiet time by herself. The last few days in college had been stressful: the student body elections were around the corner. Given the involvement of some political parties in student bodies recently, the stakes were high, and so were tempers. Some of the student candidates wanted to campaign in her classroom with elements that clearly looked like gundas. She had refused to allow it, despite their insistence. They did not cross any limits within the college premises, but it had been quite unpleasant all the same.

At about 11 a.m., the Andheri-bound slow local was nearing its penultimate station, Vile Parle. It was due to stop in another two or three minutes. The driver and guard were looking forward to some chai at Andheri station, which would be in another five to seven minutes. But the train slowed on its own, rapidly decelerated and came to a halt, its wheels screeching.

'*Aaila, slow train mein kaun chain kheencha* (Who pulled the chain in a slow train)?' the driver wondered, peering out of the open door of the motor coach, looking for answers.

The guard, who had already jumped out of the train, beat him to it.

'*Aye ruk jaao.* Stop! Stop!' he shouted after two men who were running very fast, away from the train. From their speed, and from the ease with which they jumped across the train tracks, it was obvious that they had done this several times before. One of them was not wearing pants nor any footwear. Also, judging from their location, they had probably jumped out of the ladies' compartment.

'*Saala pickpocket! Itna kya ghai tha* (What was the great rush)?' he wondered. They could have waited for the train to reach Vile Parle, and then run off. Someone had probably caught them in the act. The guard decided to go and see what the issue was. He had to; it was his job. He broke into a trot towards the ladies' compartment. The few passengers in the compartment right next to the motor coach were also peering out, looking this way and that, as were others, up and down the train. The pickpockets had probably jumped out of the second ladies' compartment that was located at the other end of the train, the guard deduced. The sun was blazing, and he hated having to run in the heat. But the next train would come along soon, so he had to make this quick to ensure the other trains did not get delayed. He kept up his trot. Nearly breathless, he still had two more compartments to cover when he heard the shrieks—wordless shouts of untold terror. They seemed to be coming from a compartment further ahead. He broke into a sprint. Something was terribly wrong. The screaming and shouting seemed to grow in volume as he moved closer and willed himself to run even faster. He finally reached the last compartment, and nearly fell over at the sight of all that blood.

The police got there half an hour later. Several men from the Railway Police and the Vile Parle station of the Mumbai Police were soon thronging the platform. They all saw the same sight as the guard—a woman had been stabbed to death in a first-class ladies' compartment seat.

She had been stabbed over and over. Blood poured out of her in streams and pooled all over the compartment floor. Apparently, she had been the only occupant of the compartment. Her red-and-orange cotton sari and matching blouse were knifed in several places, but were largely intact. No bag, no wallet, no jewellery. One slipper was still on her foot, the other lay some distance away.

There was blood everywhere—pools of it on the grimy steel floor, blood-stained palm marks and fingerprints on the seats, door handles and handrails of the compartment. The fingerprint experts collected samples. There were several prints, and they were sure to have a busy few days.

The autopsy reported that there were thirty-five stab wounds on her body. This woman had clearly put up a fight. Very likely, there had been more than one assailant—the guard and a few passengers on the train confirmed there had been at least two. No one had heard her screaming for help, so in all likelihood, someone had clamped her mouth shut. An identity card revealed her to be college professor Shanta Devi. The picture matched her face; the name on the ID card matched the one on the railway pass.

The police team at the site fanned out to look for other evidence. Presently, one constable announced with a guffaw, 'We may have a naked murderer running around. Look what I found!'

He had found a pair of blood-soaked black pants lying near the compartment door. Next to the pants, they also found a black, strappy leather chappal which showed signs of having been repaired. One of the criminals had peeled off his blood-soaked pants before running off into the slum adjoining the tracks. His chappal had probably slipped off in his haste. All of these items were added to the evidence bag. The corpse was placed in a body bag and sent off for a post-mortem.

It had been over two hours since the train had been stopped, so even if the criminals had run into the slum near the tracks, they were unlikely to be there now. Even then, a few policemen were sent to the slum to make inquiries and look for any additional clues. The Railway Police worked in tandem by making inquiries among other passengers on the local train.

News of the heinous crime had to be shared with senior officers, the press and, most importantly, with Shanta Devi's family.

According to the protocol, the investigating team prepared a press note and shared it with the newswires and major news publications. Murders always attract a lot of interest from the media, but the brutal, unprovoked murder of a young college professor in broad daylight on a Mumbai local, the main artery of the city's economic life, had the media up in arms. It made the front page in every city newspaper. Editorials and opinion pieces everywhere were livid about how the police and administration had failed to provide basic security to the city's most vulnerable population. But it was not all negative press for the police. Some journalists expressed faith that the 'world's second best police force' would surely solve the case soon enough, and regain public trust. This felt a little like reverse psychology and put more pressure on the police.

In response, senior officers like deputy commissioner (Railways), Y.C. Pawar, started to take a direct interest in the case. He wanted complete focus on its early resolution, and expected daily updates till the case was solved.

Shanta Devi's husband, Mr Narayana, resolved to do his own bit to get justice. At first, he gave angry interviews to the press, criticizing the failure of the Mumbai Police. Soon, the issue attracted political attention; it was raised in the Maharashtra state legislature. This was highly unusual, but given the sensitivity of the issue across class and caste boundaries, all parties were in agreement. This case needed early resolution to restore the people's faith in the administration's handling of law and order. Newspapers were the kings of the media world in those days, and day after day, they carried politicians, media figures and celebrities' criticism of the police, highlighting the concern about women's safety in public spaces.

As the days passed with no resolution in sight, the case began to receive even more attention. Citizens feared that the killers may strike again. 'Was it even safe for women to go to work anymore?' they asked. Those who followed Delhi's 'Nirbhaya' case in 2012 would know what I mean.

Eventually, the chief minister of Maharashtra, A.R. Antulay, in an unprecedented move, announced a ten-thousand-rupee reward for anyone who helped to solve the case.

This gave fresh fuel to the media engine. The case made headlines all over again in all major newspapers. Posters appeared at train stations announcing this reward or part thereof for anyone who provided vital clues. It was as though Mumbai was putting its entire might behind the search for the criminals. The news of the reward and the posters soon reached the slum that the criminals were last seen disappearing into. Policemen made several rounds of the area, and occasionally picked up someone or the other on suspicious grounds. But nothing stuck.

In those days, Mr Julio Ribeiro, who would later become the commissioner of the Mumbai Police, was the deputy inspector general of the Railway Police and had personally taken up the investigation of this case. The Railway Police picked up some suspects, including a man called Munna. He was a known offender in some crimes committed on trains, and this fit his modus operandi. But they were not able to find any evidence against him. This was an education in patience, and a reminder of the old maxim that not a single innocent should be punished.

*

I had learned this lesson early on in my own career, during a case in the beautiful palace of Aundh, near Pune. The palace was famous for its collection of Raja Ravi Varma's paintings. In 1973, there was a robbery, and valuables worth sixteen lakh rupees (for perspective, gold prices have risen about 200 times since then) were stolen. It was a crime suited for a top-notch detection officer, and a reputed deputy commissioner of police (DCP) was asked to come in. I too was asked to join the team. At the scene of the crime, we found an abandoned lungi. A small piece of meat was stuck to the lungi. This pointed the finger of suspicion towards the butcher, Ismail, who worked at the palace. He was arrested.

The DCP in charge, however, followed a rather unscientific practice. If his investigation pointed to a particular solution or to a particular suspect, he would 'submit this hypothesis' to an idol of Pandharpur's Lord Vithoba that he carried everywhere. He sat in front of the idol with his eyes closed, waiting for the God to give him a 'sign'. If he received the 'appropriate sign', he would be sure that his hypothesis was correct. It would be hard for one to change his mind then—it was their word against God's.

On this occasion, he submitted the hypothesis that Ismail, the butcher, was the culprit. And Lord Vithoba 'gave the sign'. After that, the DCP was convinced that Ismail was the culprit, and insisted that he confess. Ismail refused and produced a pretty solid alibi. But the DCP would not back off. He tried several means to make him confess. No luck. At some point, my persistent dissent with this approach led to my being removed from the case. Later, Ismail was transferred to a Mumbai jail. But he never yielded, and the case remained unsolved.

That case strengthened my belief about two maxims: never to accuse a man without sufficient evidence, and to never shut my mind to other possibilities, no matter how compelling a possibility might seem.

*

Weeks turned to months, and other cases and headlines took over people's attention and imagination. Gradually, Shanta Devi's case was relegated into the background of our collective consciousness. Life moved on, and the reward remained unclaimed.

About two years after the murder, in 1982, I was transferred to the Crime Investigation Department (CID) and put in charge of the case. It was an honour and an exciting posting. Here was my chance to crack a storied case that had not yielded to several competent detectives. Solving it would certainly be a feather in my cap, and it would be hugely satisfying.

I studied the case materials and evidence closely. There was a lot of material, but the only real clue was the pair of pants now caked in dried blood, and a single leather chappal that had been carefully repaired. These were both stored in the evidence bag. I opened it carefully with gloved hands, to find that by now, there was no smell at all. The pants were a little stiff in parts that had soaked in more blood. I scanned the pockets and the lining for clues. Any receipts or tags that may have been overlooked, or which spoke to me. The pants told me nothing about who had worn them.

After a few days, more current cases and other pressing matters took over my mind-space. That was, until about three months later, when a watch thief's love story intersected with my work life.

Most criminals have a modus operandi (MO). If they succeed in executing a crime with that MO, they are usually quick to repeat it. So, a gang of urban dacoits successful in looting an empty home when its occupants are at work or away will repeat the MO several times. Even they like a scalable operating model.

Petty criminals like pickpockets and chain snatchers also tend to rely on an MO. Once they identify a target victim-set, like office-goers rushing to work or women commuters on trains at, say, Churchgate station, they target them repeatedly. These days, social engineers targeting elderly people for their bank debit card pins also have an MO—it's the secret to their success.

We caught one such 'successful' watch thief, Sudhakar. Now this man was a seasoned criminal, but he was also a romantic.

In those days, most people wore an Indian watch brand like HMT. You could get simple wind-up watches for a couple of hundred rupees. During the 1980s, these and other local watch brands were popular among Mumbai's office-goers. Japanese brands like Seiko and Citizen or Swiss brands like Rado were expensive and hard to come by, because they had to be smuggled in or imported at a high cost. It could take months to get one from a place like Manish Market or Heera Panna. The streets opposite HSBC's branch in Fort were lined with illicit vendors surreptitiously selling smuggled or stolen watches. If you walked up to them for any reason to browse the innocuous looking T-shirts or caps they were displaying, they took it as a sign that you were looking for some hot goods and quickly pushed back a T-shirt or cap to give you a glance at their wares. It was a shady but lucrative business. Thieves like Sudhakar were a low-cost source of such wares.

Sudhakar had figured out an MO to identify a genuine watch, and a way of slipping it off the wearer's wrist in crowded trains and buses. Once he had it, he would slip it on his own wrist. He could easily hide three–four watches under a full-sleeved shirt.

One afternoon, at about 5 p.m., I was sitting at my desk in the CID office when I noticed a couple of constables arguing with and berating a rather dishevelled and scruffy-looking man, who turned out to be this Sudhakar.

'*Saale, har ek ghadi nikaal* (Hand over every watch). We know they are all stolen!' a constable exclaimed, handling him roughly.

'*Nahin sahab, sach bol rela hai* (No sir, I'm telling the truth)! I am handing over ten Japanese brand watches to you. Why would I lie about one desi HMT watch? *Sachchi*, my wife gifted it to me. Please don't take this one watch,' he was pleading with the cops.

Petty criminals are frequently arrested, and therefore, quite practised at hoodwinking the constables who arrest them. This pair of constables was not so gullible.

In response to his pleas, Sudhakar got a whack from a police lathi. He yowled loudly in pain.

'Saab, saab! I am really not lying. *Maa kasam* (I swear upon my mother)!'

Something in the way he spoke made me want to believe him. Besides, since Sudhakar had confessed, and we had found so much of his loot, we were sure to get a conviction. We did not really need that one watch he seemed to hold dear, to strengthen our case. On the off-chance that he was speaking the truth, Sudhakar did deserve to have what was his.

I walked up to the door of my room, and called out to the constables,

'*Aat ana tyala* (Bring him in).'

When they did, I asked the constables to let go of Sudhakar and addressed him directly.

'What do you want?'

'Saab, I agree I have stolen these watches. There are seventeen in total. Mostly imported. I am an expert at opening the Seiko and Citizen metal strap clasps. I accept my crime and will do so in court too. I am giving over all the stolen goods. My only request is that you not confiscate this steel HMT watch. This is a wedding gift from my wife. She used to work at a small office before we got married, and she bought this for me from her own earnings. Please don't confiscate it.'

'Okay,' I said tersely.

The constables took him away. Later, when the case papers were being prepared, I instructed the officers to not include that HMT watch in the list. Instead, I had it put away in our storage room, marked as the personal property of Sudhakar while he was in prison.

Sudhakar was sentenced to six months. After completing his sentence, he was required to report daily at the police station he had been arrested in for the next month. On what was probably the third or fourth day of his visit, I saw him waiting to mark his attendance with the head constable.

'*Arre* Sudhakar, *tum chhoot bhi gaya* (You have been released already)? Did you take your watch yet?'

'*Salaam, saab*! Why are you teasing me? What watch?'

I reminded him of our conversation when he was arrested.

'*Saab, mereko toh sab yaad hai* (Of course, I remember it all)! But I am very surprised that you remember. My wife is very sad that the watch is gone.'

'But Sudhakar, the watch is not gone. It's still with us.'

I told one of the constables to take Sudhakar to the storeroom so he could claim what was his.

Half an hour later, Sudhakar was back at my desk.

'*Saab, shukriya Saab*.'

'Did you get your watch?' I asked, even though I could see a steel strap on his left wrist quite clearly.

'Yes, saab. Thank you, saab. I cannot believe that you did this for me saab. Thank you very much saab.'

'*Koi baat nahin* (no worries), this was just basic humanity. No one else has claimed it anyway. Now stop stealing and stay out for a few months with your wife.'

'Saab, I will remember your kindness, and repay it one day,' he vowed.

I didn't have to wait long. Three days later, I walked into the office to find Sudhakar waiting for me.

'Namaste, saab!'

'Namaste. What have you done now?'

'Nothing, saab. I have come to repay my debt to you.'

'Achha? How is that?'

'*Aapko ek khabar dena hai* (I want to give you a tip).'

'About what?'

'About the murder on that train, of Professor Shanta Devi.'

My jaw dropped in astonishment. That case had been given up as unsolved. What could this watch thief possibly tell me?

'Come in. And if this is *bhankas* (rubbish), *yaad rakhna*. Just watch.'

'The news is reliable, saab. It is first-hand. I can tell you who killed her and where you can catch him.'

I could not believe my ears and my good luck.

'Sit and tell me what you know.'

'Saab, my house is close to those tracks. You know that the man who committed the murder threw his pants on the tracks before running away. He then ran straight to my house. We are both old criminals and know each other from the trade. That day I was home—I had just finished doing the rounds of the morning buses and was eating my breakfast when Qayoom ran into my house in his underwear. He was panting and could barely talk.

'"Lun...lun...lungi. Give ... me a lungi" is all he managed to say,' Sudhakar acted out. 'I asked him, "*Kya baat hai* (What's the matter), Qayoom? Have you scored early in the morning today?" He replied, "*Haan, yaar*. It was a good morning. But it got quite messy."'

Sudhakar continued, 'He then told me the grisly events of that morning. Qayoom said he boarded that local train, intending to rob the lone woman in the first-class compartment. He thought it would be easy to scare her and told her to hand over her jewellery. He even showed her a knife. He thought she would get scared and hand it over. He didn't have much time. They had boarded her train at Santacruz and had to get down before the next station. But the woman refused to listen. She started to shout. He said they had no option, and he had to use his knife to stab her. But he had gone overboard, and there was a lot of blood. They jumped off the train before it fully stopped and ran. Qayoom could not run in his blood-soaked pants. So he threw them on the tracks.

'I was aghast at what he had done. I had known him to be a thief like me, but he had committed what sounded like a brutal murder. But he had no regrets. It was like he was on a high. He even showed me the four gold bangles that he had stolen from her.

'I figured the best way to get him out of my house was to give him that lungi. I did, and cursorily asked him what he planned to do next. I felt sure the police would not let a daylight murder go unpunished. Qayoom said he was not worried, and was going to disappear for some time. He planned to go to his village, Shendurni, near Jalgaon. He felt he had enough money to tide him over for a few months. But he sternly warned me against revealing what he had told me, and his plans.

'I did not see him after that. But I have heard he works in his uncle's cycle shop in Shendurni.

'When your policemen came to make inquiries in my area, I lied to them that I did not know about the murder. I had no reason to help you guys. But what you have done for me means a lot, so I want to help you.'

'This is great information, Sudhakar,' I said. 'We will follow this thread. But if you are lying, I am warning you again. You will be an accomplice to a murder—twice over. Then your wife will not see the watch or you.'

'Try me,' Sudhakar replied defiantly, before his voice turned sombre. 'One more thing, you cannot mention the lungi to Qayoom. If he or anyone else asks you how you found that he was involved, you cannot mention me. I will deny it, and you will never see me again—at least not alive.'

The information that Sudhakar gave me was very specific. I called our deputy commissioner to seek his approval for the next course of action.

'Sudhakar's story is hard to ignore, sir. I think we should send a team to Jalgaon and check out his information,' I said.

'Zende, you are being naive. He is a petty watch thief. He is probably trying to prank us because he had to spend six months in jail,' said the DCP.

'I don't think so, sir. He had no reason to lie in this situation. He volunteered this information privately to me after I helped him. Although a seasoned watch thief, Sudhakar has a zameer (conscience). Otherwise, he would not have been so particular about his wife's gift,' I replied.

'I still have my doubts, Zende,' said the DCP.

'Sir, Qayoom is a habitual offender. He has even served time in the past. There is reasonable cause to believe he could be involved. Besides, all we are doing is sending two policemen for a couple of days. If they come back empty handed, no one needs to know. But if we do make an arrest, it will be a big badge of honour for the Mumbai Police. This was a high-visibility case. People will be happy to know that we did not let go of our man even after such a long time.'

'*Theek aahe* (okay), Zende. Let's do this. Good luck!'

It was a swift operation. The team easily located the cycle shop that Qayoom worked at in Shendurni. When he saw the cops, Qayoom did not flinch; he just asked why he was being arrested now. He declared his innocence in the matter, but did not resist. He had been arrested before and was familiar with what came next. He also knew that the police had to work very hard to get him convicted, especially for such a serious crime.

With the help of the local police, our team searched Qayoom's home and belongings to collect evidence, especially the bangles. Nothing came up. We were taking this man from Jalgaon to Mumbai solely on the basis of some information we had received from Sudhakar, a convicted watch thief. We were on thin ice.

Qayoom was brought back to Mumbai in an overnight train and remanded to police custody. I met him the next morning. He had the furtive, shifty eyes of a hunted man. They were a little red from a sleepless night in a jail cell. He was not fat, but he had the paunch of a man who took long naps after heavy meals. He was wearing a pair of work pants, soiled with cycle grease, and an old, similarly stained grey T-shirt with a faded image of Amitabh Bachchan from his role as a dock worker in *Deewar*.

'*Kya saab. Kaiko laya humko idhar? Apun koi murder-birder nahin kiya hai* (Sir, why have you brought me here? I have not killed anyone).'

'Since when have you been in Jalgaon?'

'About two years.'

'So, right after committing the murder, you ran away.'

'*Nahin, saab*. Is it a crime to go visit your family? After my last time in jail, I decided to give up this life. But I could not find any work. No one wants to hire a convict. So, I finally went back to my town, and I am living hand-to-mouth.'

'We will see about that.'

'Constable, open the evidence bag. Take out that chappal.'

Qayoom slipped on the chappal that the constable gave him. It fit perfectly.

'*Kya, saab.* Half the men in Mumbai probably wear the same size chappals. How can this be mine?'

We then made him try on the pants, still caked with the dried blood of Prof. Shanta Devi. They were tight around the waist and butt. But that could easily be due to the weight he had gained in two years. Qayoom kept riding his luck.

'*Dekha, saab,* this is not mine. *Aap khaali-peeli apun ko ghaseet raha hai* (You're unnecessarily dragging me into this).'

'*Chori ka kha kha ke mota ho gaya* (You've gotten fat on eating the proceeds of theft),' I retorted.

We interrogated him for a couple of hours, but he would not let on. We put him away for the day and then another night or two. But he did not change his stance. We tried several means, but had no luck. Time was running out. We could not keep him in jail indefinitely without charging him, but for that we needed some evidence against him.

Several times, I was tempted to tell him the story of the lungi, and how we knew about his involvement. But I had given my word, and that was more important than getting a conviction.

With just a couple of days to go before we would have to release him, I sat by myself at my desk with the only two pieces of evidence in front of me: the chappal and the blood-stained pants. The pants were lying stretched out on the table. I had looked at them closely, pockets and all. Despite the blood, they had not yielded any fingerprints. I picked up the chappal again. There were no brand markings anywhere. Its sole had probably come apart at some time and had been stitched back together along the outer edge. Could these stitches be the clue? I remembered reading in a Sherlock Holmes story how each craftsman often has his own signature style, much like a criminal's MO. A humble roadside cobbler may not strike one as a craftsman, but in reality, he is. There was a chance that this was someone's signature stitch.

There's a Marathi saying—*Adla Hari gadhavache pai dhari*—meaning, even God, when faced with an intractable problem, might seek the help of a donkey.

It was a really long shot, but we had no better leads. I called in Sub-Inspector Bawiskar early the following day.

'Where did Qayoom stay when he was in Mumbai?'

'Last we know, he was in Vikhroli, saab. In Parksite jhopadpatti (slum). He also confirmed that during questioning.'

'Very good. This is what you will do today: take this chappal, keep it carefully in a transparent plastic bag, so you don't lose it or damage the evidence. You can see that the sole has been stitched back. Go to every cobbler who sits in that jhopadpatti and within a one-kilometre radius. Pay extra attention to important areas like near bus stops, or hawker stalls, or the road to the train station. Show them this stitching, and ask them if they did it.'

Bawiskar was incredulous, but mustered the courage to speak up. '*Kai, saheb?* How is it possible? How can a cobbler recognize a chappal like this? That too two years old?'

I put on my most convincing tone, what you'd now call 'fake it till you make it', and said, 'Don't you know every cobbler has his characteristic style of stitching? The right one, if he is still there, is sure to recognize it. Make sure you cover the entire area today. Take some constables along. We can keep Qayoom in remand for only two more days.'

Bawiskar complied. I was his boss after all. Besides, I had the reputation for knowing this city well.

They were back a little after 2 p.m., sweating from a day spent walking in Mumbai's sweltering heat, but excitedly nudging along their new companion—Tukaram Shinde. Tukaram Shinde was a cobbler who worked out of a shed in Vikhroli's vast Parksite slum. Uncharacteristically for a roadside cobbler, his white loose pyjama was very clean, apart from a few permanent-looking stains of shoe polish. He wore a pastel green cotton shirt, and the soft white cotton cap typical of Marathi people. He had a neatly drawn gandha—a thumb-sized mark made with vermilion—on his forehead. He could have been a man from Zendewadi, the village I grew up in.

'Saheb, this is Tukaram. His tapri is in the same slum where Qayoom lived. He recognizes the stitching on Qayoom's chappal. In fact, he remembers Qayoom very well,' Sub-Inspector Bawiskar announced. Clearly, he was still surprised that this strategy had worked, but was nevertheless brimming with excitement at the thought that we may have finally cracked this high-profile case.

'*Ae, saang re Tukaram* (Tell me, Tukaram),' I said, directing him to speak.

'*Ho, saheb.* I have stitched this chappal,' said Tukaram, clearly a man of few words.

'How can you be so sure? When did you do it?'

'It was about two or two-and-a-half years ago, I remember clearly.'

'You remember every chappal you stitch?'

'*Naahi saheb.* But I cannot forget the owner of this chappal. He is a big sheth, a rich and generous man.'

This sounded even better than what I had imagined. 'Why do you remember the man?'

'Saheb, in our slum, people fuss over every paisa they pay. They can buy a chappal from a roadside stall for five or six rupees. Three years ago, on Eid, the owner of this chappal came to get his chappal polished. He loved the job I had done and gave me twenty-five rupees for the job. Said it was my Eid gift. Who else but a sheth can be so generous? And how can I, a poor cobbler, forget him? I remember him very well. I remember stitching this a few months later.'

I could scarcely believe my ears. This man could be the answer to all our efforts and prayers.

I asked for Qayoom to be brought out.

Tired after spending six days in police custody, Qayoom shuffled out of his cell. He shrugged off the grip of the constable who, in his excitement, was dragging him along. Qayoom appeared to vaguely recognize this man, dressed in traditional-looking Marathi clothes.

Tukaram, on the other hand, was shocked. He could not believe his sheth was in such bad shape, and in police custody. But he was very clear.

'Yes, saheb. This is my sheth. I can never forget him. He is the one who gave me the Eid gift, and whose chappal this is.'

Qayoom crumpled to the ground. He knew his game was up. A pillar of stubborn resistance for the last six days, he was now a bawling mess on the floor. Squatting on the floor, he shouted in agony, '*Maaf kar do, saab. Galti ho gaya* (Forgive me, sir, it was a mistake)! *Saab, maaf kar do* ... *Saab, maaf kar do* ... I did not intend to kill her, I only wanted to steal the bangles.'

Once he knew he had been recognized, Qayoom lost all his strength and confessed to everything. His version largely matched the story we already knew.

Mumbai local trains' first-class compartments are usually empty after peak hours. Given the high price of a first-class ticket, only well-paid office-goers or well-heeled students ride in these compartments. Qayoom and a couple of his hangers-on patrolled the stations to spot any lone traveller who might be a potential target for theft. They would wait surreptitiously, board the ladies' compartment, either by climbing in from the track-side entrance, or jumping aboard from the platform side just as the train pulled out of the station.

That day, there were two of them, Qayoom and Munna. They were watching the trains go by at Santacruz station. They saw Shanta Devi sitting at the window, peering out, her chin resting on her palm, watching the world go past. Two bangles shone at the base of her forearm. The other arm probably had two more, they inferred. Four gold bangles were a lot. And since she travelled first class, they were probably real gold, not fake. It was hard to tell these days, even for experts like Qayoom.

Munna quickly got into the adjoining compartment and jumped off on to the tracks on the other side. He climbed the steps of the women's compartment but did not enter. No one seemed to notice, or care. Qayoom quickly went to the end of the platform, and just as the train pulled out, he jumped into the ladies' first-class compartment. They had about six to seven minutes to complete their job and jump off the train before it entered the next station, Vile Parle. A simple chain pull usually did the trick whenever they were done and ready to bolt—provided the chain was working. They had to trust their luck on this one.

They swiftly got to work. Shanta Devi was looking out of the window and did not see them enter. The clatter of the train's movement on the tracks ensured she did not hear them tiptoe to her either. Qayoom approached her from the front, while Munna slipped into the adjoining set of seats behind her. To keep it quick, Qayoom pulled out his knife, and pointed to her jewellery, and asked her to hand it all over to him.

The professor made to jump up, as if to escape. One man's hand clasped over her mouth, and another pulled her back and pinned her to the seat. She kicked at Qayoom. Given that she was wearing a sari, she could not move her legs about too much, and barely grazed Qayoom's leg. But this pushed him over the edge. He stabbed her once, twice, three times in the abdomen. Blood sprayed forth onto his pants . But she kicked again.

By now, Qayoom was in a frenzy. This had not been his plan. She was supposed to meekly hand over her jewellery. He stabbed her wildly now, in her arms, shoulder, stomach, face ... he could not stop! This woman had ruined his simple plan—it was all her fault! She had long stopped resisting, but her blood kept flowing out in spurts and sprays. His pants were drenched in blood, and he felt sick. This made him angrier; this woman had even ruined his pants now. His head was ready to explode with mad rage. He heard a voice in the distance; telling him to stop, because the woman was apparently dead.

Qayoom regained enough sense to pull off her bangles. This was the jackpot, and it had to be his. The other man took the thin gold chain around her neck, and the contents of her now overturned bag. Qayoom pulled the emergency chain. The 10.14 a.m. Andheri slow train from Churchgate ground to a halt just a little before Vile Parle station. Qayoom and Munna jumped off and ran in the direction of the slums. Qayoom peeled off his blood-soiled pants and rid himself of the unpleasant memory of that woman. One chappal came off in his haste, but he let it drop. When it became difficult to run with just one chappal on, he took the other one off too, but did not throw it. It had cost him almost fifty rupees, plus the twenty-five he had gifted that cobbler in a fit of generosity.

He reached the houses on the outskirts of the slum now, and continued to run, looking quite crazy in his full-sleeved shirt and underwear. He could not go anywhere dressed like this. He could not even see any clothes drying nearby. He knew a man who stayed here though, an ordinary watch thief. Qayoom could not remember his name. But Qayoom remembered that the man loved his wife too much and got very touchy if someone made a lewd comment about her. He would surely have some pants to lend. And if Qayoom threatened to harm his wife, he would keep shut about the incident. Qayoom found his house easily. He was lounging in a lungi, outside his house, a glass of chai in his hand.

In about two minutes, Qayoom had threatened him into giving him a lungi and walked away hurriedly, trying his best to not break into a run. No one was chasing him anymore. In his haste and confusion, he had probably revealed more than he should have to that guy who gave him the lungi. Why couldn't he remember his name?

Qayoom did not waste much time after that. He quickly went home, laid low for a couple of days to ensure no one was looking for him, and then sold the bangles to a couple of jewellers who were known not to ask too many questions. Then, he fled to Jalgaon.

Purged of the burden of guilt he had been carrying, Qayoom fell into an exhausted silence.

In two weeks, the Shanta Devi murder had gone from a two-year-old cold case to the main perpetrator confessing to his crime. And all this because of a small gesture of kindness towards a petty watch thief.

We sent our report to the senior officers. Ribeiro, who was by now additional commissioner, could not believe it. He decided to come over and interrogate Qayoom himself. This was highly unusual. But our detection had been rock-solid and Qayoom was charged with the unprovoked murder of Professor Shanta Devi by stabbing. Munna too was rearrested and charged. Our team won the Chief Minister's Award of 10,000 rupees.

I wanted to thank the cobbler Tukaram Shinde, who had played such a vital role in this success and share our reward with him. So, I called him to our office and asked him to name his reward. Tukaram politely declined the offer.

'What reward, saheb. I only stated a simple truth. It was no big deal,' he said.

'But Tukaram, your simple truth was so valuable for us. Accept something. Allow us to show our gratitude,' I insisted.

'*Ek chaha paaja* (Buy me a cup of tea),' he said.

I was struck by the simplicity of his gesture, and his humility, but thought it best not to insist any more. So, I offered him a chair, and we waited for the chai. While waiting, I noticed that he was wearing a tulshimaal.

'Are you a varkari?' I asked him excitedly.

'*Haan, saheb*, I don't miss my Pandurang darshan,' he replied, reverentially touching his ears.

'So, every year, you stand in the heat for eight to ten hours, waiting for darshan?'

'Yes, saheb.'

'Okay, I will give you a letter. Show it to the police officer on duty, and he will ensure you don't have to stand in line. You will get your darshan as a priority,' I offered, glad for being able to pay him back in some way.

Tukaram categorically refused and was positively upset at the suggestion.

'Saheb, Vithoba is my God. It is my honour and privilege to walk with other varkaris and wait in line with them for my darshan. I have no desire for this favouritism in Pandharpur,' Tukaram declared.

I was amazed. Even a man who appeared to be a poor cobbler lived with such piety. He seemed free from desire. Such devotion could only be found in a living saint. I rose from my chair and literally prostrated at his feet.

2

THE DEADLY RIOTS OF PYDHONIE

In the heart of south Mumbai, at the mouth of the narrow Ibrahim Merchant street, stands a beautiful 250-year-old mosque with high, ornate minarets, called the Minara Masjid. The often-crowded street where it stands is home to over 400 eateries that serve delectable Mughlai and Awadhi food: nalli nihari from Delhi, biryanis from Lucknow, tawa chicken from Bahraich in Uttar Pradesh.[2] Little wonder then that during the holy month of Ramzan, its adjoining streets and Mohammed Ali Road, attract over one lakh visitors every day, of which only a quarter are Muslim. Google 'iftaar eateries in Mumbai', and all the top search results have one address: Minara Masjid.

2 'Covid-19: Mumbai's Mohammed Ali road, with 250-year history, might be desolate this Ramzan', Live Mint, 19 April 2020, https://www.livemint.com/news/india/covid-19-mumbai-s-mohammed-ali-road-with-250-year-history-might-be-desolate-this-ramzan-11587298047444.html

Suleiman Mithaiwala, in this area, is still our family's go-to place for the best phirni, a delicious rice kheer served in beautiful earthen pots.

Minara Masjid is the main mosque for the lakhs of people who live in the Pydhonie/Dongri area, one of the most densely populated places in Mumbai. The Masjid, surrounded by shops, roadside stalls and narrow lanes crammed with low-rise buildings and chaotic traffic, is an oasis of respite and serenity.

I served in that area for several years and lived in the police quarters barely a fifteen-minute walk from the Masjid for nearly thirty years. By 1992, when I served as the assistant commissioner of the Pydhonie Division, I was intimately familiar with the lanes of that area. I even won a bet to locate the signboard that displays that area's other popular name, 'Bhendi Bazaar', a challenge most people fail at.

The year 1992 saw some of the worst communal riots in Mumbai, and their aftermath across the country tore into India's social fabric. The riots were triggered on 6 December by the destruction of the Babri Masjid, a mosque 1,500 km away in Ayodhya. The dispute over the mosque had become a divisive issue in India; any activity in that region meant that police across the country went on alert and increased security in anticipation of violence.

In 1990, L.K. Advani, a senior Bharatiya Janata Party leader, started a 10,000-km Ram Rath Yatra from Somnath in Gujarat towards Ayodhya. This attracted thousands of kar sevaks to its ranks wherever it went, and there were incidents of violence along its route. People across the whole country held their collective breath in anticipation of what might happen if they all reached Ayodhya. Finally, the rath yatra was halted by the Bihar government. Thwarted in this fashion, the kar sevaks sought an alternate solution for a few months. In 1992, the matter was sub judice in the Supreme Court of India.

The kar sevals decided that 6 December 1992 would be their D-Day. One lakh people, kar sevaks, and representatives of organizations like the Vishva Hindu Parishad, the Bharatiya Janata Party, Bajrang Dal and the Mumbai-based Shiv Sena, gathered in Ayodhya near the hotly disputed Babri Masjid. Mass leaders like Advani, Murli Manohar Joshi and Uma Bharti gave powerful speeches. Television cameras were everywhere. There was heavy police presence too. Around noon, one man slipped into the cordoned-off Babri Masjid premises, climbed on top of the structure and brandished a saffron flag. Others in the crowd took that cue and attacked the mosque with axes, iron rods and grappling hooks. Soon the entire 400-year old structure collapsed in a heap. The entire country watched the violence unfold on television.

The demolition of the Babri Masjid set up the most unforgettable day of my police career. The events put hundreds of lives at risk, and truly tested the trust I had earned among the local population in the Pydhonie Division.

The Maharashtra state government was aware that any damage to the Masjid could easily trigger riots in my jurisdiction. The division included Dongri and Bhendi Bazaar—some of the most communally sensitive parts of Mumbai, where over 60 per cent of the population was Muslim. Riots periodically broke out in this area, and it was deemed to be communally sensitive. Over the years, people had died, and homes, shops and public property had been destroyed in riots. Anticipating another flare-up if the structure in Ayodhya was demolished, we had maintained preventive security in the area right from the days of the rath yatra. On 6 December 1992, after the demolition of the Babri Masjid, we ramped this up substantially.

Policemen in groups of two or three, wearing riot jackets and helmets, and carrying batons or rifles, and officers carrying service revolvers had been stationed in the most sensitive locations. Two police jeeps with one officer and four constables each were positioned at nodal locations to quickly reach any place that needed reinforcements. A wireless van was also manned round the clock with a staff of eight to ten rifle-bearing constables and jamadars, ready to swing into action in case of any major incidence of violence. Almost the entire staff of three police stations was on the streets. The senior inspectors in charge of the police stations and I continually moved between sensitive locations, our ears to the ground at all times and attentive to any wireless broadcasts in the jeeps. I had on my trusted green helmet of twenty years, and my service revolver, which fortunately had never seen action in my entire career so far. I hoped it would remain unused. We were exercising all precautions and remained optimistic that nothing untoward would happen on our watch.

Our optimism, however, was on thin ice. The Dongri area had been nothing short of a tinder box for the past few days, albeit for reasons completely unrelated to the Babri Masjid events.

Those were the days of G.R. Khairnar, the feared, incorruptible deputy commissioner of the Bombay Municipal Corporation (now Brihanmumbai Municipal Corporation). He was best known for relentlessly demolishing illicit construction across the city.

Mumbai had several with illegal commercial and residential structures, big and small. Some of the owners could not navigate the bureaucracy to acquire valid licences; others did not bother to. They relied instead on the goons' and government servants' hafta (protection money) networks to get by. As these kutcha and pucca structures proliferated, they not only became an eyesore, but also blocked streets, and became a safety and security hazard—a complete civic nightmare. Even when the Bombay Municipal Corporation scheduled a demolition of these illicit structures, the 'networks' would ensure the job was poorly executed and the shops and homes were up and running in no time.

Khairnar, however, decided to cut through the clutter, and clear all the streets of Mumbai. He would personally show up for the demolitions, sometimes without informing anyone, not even the local police. When possible, he would get the local police station to provide the required security and ensure every structure in his crosswires for demolition was truly flattened. He would brook no opposition, and all protests and criticism were silently ignored. He was simply doing his job, and doing rather well at that. So, in the eyes of the middle-class, newspaper-reading public, he was a hero. Obviously, then, the local police and the courts co-operated with him willy-nilly.

The same Khairnar had recently conducted a demolition drive in Dongri, which is a web of many, many small lanes and bylanes that have organically grown for over 150 years. Two and three-storey residential structures, like many of their residents, appear a lot older than they really are, from years of being squeezed to their maximum. The narrow lanes accommodate scores of legal and illegal street vendors and small stalls. For many in those areas, these tiny shops are their only source of income. Since big retailers and major brands rarely want to set up shop in this low-income and communally sensitive area, these small outlets fulfil the vital needs of the local community. Shoppers and passers-by on foot, motorcycles, cars, luggage-carrying carts and vans jostle for space in these lanes. The people of the area have a language that is quintessentially their own—Hindi laced with Urdu and 'Bambaiya' swear words. It is the school of the hardest knocks and counts some of Mumbai's most notorious criminals among its alumni.

In these environs, Khairnar and his team demolished hundreds of shops. The policemen had kept protesters at bay and a lot of families had lost their source of livelihood. One of the demolished stalls used to sell copies of the Holy Quran, and the people of the area felt that in demolishing the stall, Khairnar had desecrated the Holy Quran.

The news spread rapidly. Tension was running high and there was a general strike (bandh) in the area. The BEST buses had been blockaded, and to avoid any incidents of burning, services to the area had been temporarily suspended for three days now. As a result, people had lost their only source of transportation, forcing them to remain housebound and lose more money in the bargain. Consequently, they were frustrated, and the feeling of 'victimhood' was at its peak.

The Babri Masjid demolition added fuel to this simmering fire.

I had been following the developments in Ayodhya closely. We had also maintained a dialogue with the local population in our division and had our finger on the pulse of the community. In anticipation of the planned event on 6 December at Ayodhya, we brought together a few Muslim community leaders for a discussion a day earlier. The mood was sombre, but there was one reason for optimism. A local leader said, 'Sahab, we think there should be no problem. Most of us here in Mumbai are

Sunni. Babri is a Shia Mosque. Why should we care if it is destroyed?'

Some of the other leaders agreed. I had my doubts.

On the morning of 6 December, the day of the gathering at the Babri Masjid, the local municipal authorities asked my opinion on whether we should resume the bus service the following day. I suggested that we wait a little longer. They did, and that turned out to be a good decision.

The Babri Masjid fell later that same afternoon. Mobile phones were still a few years away and people relied on grainy images on the television and hearsay for updates on what was happening in Ayodhya. I had been following every news update and we continued constant patrolling. There was no question of any of us policemen going home, not even when our shifts ended. Even the State Reserve Police had been deployed. I ordered a recce of all the sensitive areas of the division. There was an uneasy calm—it felt like the calm just before the storm. Even the few shops that had opened after the bandh downed their shutters. Everyone was just watching the news updates on TV, wondering what was to happen next.

At 10.15 p.m., I got a call from a local leader of the Imamvada locality. 'Sahab, this is not fair,' he said. 'These people are bursting firecrackers here. Just because we are not saying anything and maintaining calm does not mean they can mock us like this. You need to come and stop them.'

'Don't worry. I will be there,' I said. I had to ensure that such incidents did not escalate. Going there was the best course of action, and I did just that.

We got there shortly and found five or six miscreants responsible for the incident. I talked to them politely but firmly. '*Dekho, yeh theek nahin hai* (Look, this is not right). Your neighbours are clearly hurt by today's events. If you do all this, it will only create more tension. Stop this right now. And if you do it again, *yaad rakhna* (remember my warning)!' I said. Soon, peace was restored. At least for the time being.

Around 10.30 p.m., we received a message on the wireless radio that some vehicles had been damaged near Minara Masjid—their windshields cracked, their tyres slashed. We rushed to the spot. All traffic in the area had come to a standstill because of a large crowd that had gathered there. It was easy to sense their anger and aggression. Our presence and the blaring police sirens did little to calm or intimidate them.

'*Band karo* (Stop this right now)!' I shouted at the crowd.

We repeated the announcement over the megaphone a few times. Nevertheless, the crowd refused to back down and we were forced to resort to a lathi charge—a few sharp smacks with the bamboo batons on some of the more aggressive rioters. This worked and we were able to disperse the crowd. Short respite.

In the meantime, another incident had been reported in a nearby lane and we were needed there, so we rushed off. It was important to nip any violence in the bud. The areas under Pydhonie Division are often a bellwether for how Mumbai will respond to any communally sensitive incident outside the city. The religious and community leaders of the area are very influential. If peace is maintained in this area, then the rest of Mumbai will most likely follow suit. That was part of the reason that an officer like me, who was experienced in preventing and managing communal tension, was posted to this sensitive area.

Presently, we received a message on the wireless, 'Sir, there is big trouble brewing near Minara Masjid.'

'*Parat ya* (Turn back!)!'

We rushed back there. By the time we reached Minara Masjid, a huge mob had gathered on the streets. They had blockaded the road and vandalized some cars and two or three buses. They had also turned their fury on a municipal van. Another lathi charge dispersed the mob, but it did not vanish, merely fleeing into one of the lanes. The entire area is a labyrinth of lanes and bylanes. As soon as we dispersed the mob from one lane, it reappeared in another lane. We chased after it with our lathis and it reappeared in yet another lane. It was unending, like a game of real-life whack-a-mole.

Meanwhile, in Masjid Lane nearby, the crowd started pelting stones at shops and other property. I rushed in with a big company of over twenty policemen. Soon, a gunshot rang out from one of the side lanes. I knew, from its sound, that it was not from a police weapon. A line had been crossed. We had to up our game. The bullet had hit the helmet of an officer and while he was unhurt, he was visibly shaken. More gunshots rang out from the same lane. This emboldened many others to pick up stones. Not only people on the streets, but now people from the homes and buildings on both sides of the lane joined in. Even women, elders and children probably joined the fray, hidden behind windows that opened and shut rhythmically. Stones and projectiles were hurled at us from everywhere.

Clearly, the pent-up anger of the past few days was beginning to burst forth. The people were using this as an opportunity to vent, and the police had become the face of everything that was wrong with their lives. We had to push them back and stop them for their own good—in any riot it is the local community of that area that suffers the most.

We released some tear gas into the crowds, filling the air with thick smoke, and the sounds of angry shouting and glass breaking were quickly replaced by those of men coughing and wheezing. The stones eased up, but only briefly. The rioters were in a frenzy and getting more aggressive every minute. We had only one option left now.

I ordered our armed constables to line up. There were only five of them and they were carrying old, but effective and imposing-looking rifles. They loaded their rifles, rested the heavy wooden butts against their shoulders, and pointed the barrels up in the air.

The megaphone blasted a peremptory warning, '*Ruk jao, varna hum goli chalayenge* (Stop now, or we will open fire)!' More stones came our way.

'Fire!' I commanded.

Five shots rang out as one. Even in the frenzied cacophony of hundreds of rioters, the report of five .303 bullets can freeze blood. The determined crack echoed in the narrow lane. The stones eased up. Five more shots rang out from our rifles. The crowd knew we were serious. But the men seemed to be in the grip of insanity and instigated by faceless leaders who continued to goad them on: '*Maaro! Police kuchh nahi kar sakti* (Don't stop, the police can't do anything)!' Who knew whether these were aggrieved residents of these areas or just lumpen characters trying to further their own evil intentions? They seemed to blend in with the crowd and knew how to push their buttons. Firing is the strongest weapon that police have access to. Usually, the sound of bullets fired in the air scares and stops rioting mobs.

This time, with the rioters refusing to back down, I ordered the constables to lower their rifles to shoulder level and aim for their legs. But the people in the mob were continually bending down to find and pick up stones, or were stumbling over one another in the melee. We could not control where the bullets actually struck. Shrieks from the injured rent the air. But it did not stop the mob. Five more bullets were fired. Still no effect. Five more. This was the hardest part of my job as a policeman: shooting at the very people I had sworn to protect. But sometimes, you have to take some stern steps to protect the larger good—the city and its people. Despite my years of experience, such use of force was very stressful, and my heart was thumping rapidly, ready to explode in my chest. However, with each beat, my mind gained clarity. *Nodwijetprapya chapriyam* (Don't be upset by adverse events)—this shloka from the Bhagavad Gita popped into my mind. Even if unpleasant, I was doing my duty as a policeman in the best possible way. All my senses were fully alert. I could see the people who fell, their friends dragging them, carrying them away. The goading shouts had gradually switched from '*maaro* (hit/kill)!' to '*ruk jao, bhago mat* (stop, don't run away)!'

The rioters, unsure whom the next volley of shots would hit, ran helter-skelter, and the violence eased. Relief! We stayed put, ready for any repeat action.

Two people had died in the firing, and some others were injured. We called for ambulances from J.J. Hospital to attend to the dead and the injured. A few people lingered on the streets in groups of three or four, but they were just watching—for the time being, at least. Having restored a precarious calm, I headed back to my post, leaving two policemen behind to keep watch.

The tension lasted till about midnight. We put down several minor incidents in the meantime. We extinguished a couple of fires and thwarted an attempt to set a truck on fire near the Shani Temple. By about 2.30 or 3 a.m., things had quietened down, and we got a much-needed breather. We figured that we had till about 6 a.m. Any action would probably start only after that. We organized our security and police posts in anticipation of what was to come.

The next morning dawned clear and quiet. It was as if the previous day's skirmishes had never happened. People had probably expected much worse from Dongri after a major incident like the Babri Masjid demolition, but when that did not happen, most resumed their routine, going about their day like any other. Around 9 a.m., shops had begun to open. It seemed like it would be business as usual. The BEST buses were still off the road, but other traffic moved about freely.

This peace did not last long, and soon cracks began to appear in the seemingly smooth surface.

An hour or so later, a small group of about ten to fifteen men in their teens and twenties gathered on Mohammed Ali Road. Perhaps they were unemployed and had nothing better to do; perhaps they had an ulterior motive for gathering in this fashion. They blockaded the road with broken fencing, stones from construction debris and uprooted road dividers, and stopped all vehicles from passing through the area.

'*Aaj hamara area bandh hai* (Today, our area is closed)!' they announced. I figured that there was probably some residual tension from the previous day's events that these men needed to vent. So, instead of using coercion to rein them in, I asked traffic to be diverted away from that area. We asked for State Reserve Police reinforcements and posted them in the more violence-prone areas like Masjid Lane and in central locations like J.J. Junction, just in case things got out of hand.

Around 11 a.m., more men joined the group, and the mob soon began to swell. Standing around in large groups, some of them began to get combative, directing their aggression against the police presence. 'We don't want you cops here. *Chale jaao yahan se* (go away from here). Our mosque was broken in Ayodhya. Why didn't you go there to protect the mosque? Why have you come here? Go away. Our area is closed today.'

Gradually, a mob of about one hundred people picked that up as a chant. '*Aaj area bandh hai! Aaj area bandh hai!*'

We stayed close to the groups but did not stop them from protesting. We had cordoned off the crowd, so they would not spill out to other areas.

Then someone hurled a tennis-ball-sized stone. The stone hit a Marwari-owned shop's glass window, and it came down with a loud crash. An even louder victory roar rose from that group. The trembling shop owner hurriedly downed his shutter. The mob had tasted blood, and soon, a competition seemed to start among the gathered groups of men, intent on violence—each wanted to one-up the others in wreaking havoc and destruction. Several shops owned by Hindu businessmen were targeted and broken. We made announcements asking the rioters to stop, warned them, even lathi charged them. All to no avail.

By now the crowd was huge, about 300–400 people armed with sticks, stones, planks, iron rods, knives, sickles, etc. There was a pretty good chance that at least some of them were carrying kerosene or diesel and were ready to start fires. People were now streaming in from all directions to join the mob, mostly young men in their teens to thirties. They were all ordinary people—labourers, students, blue- and white-collar workers and shop-owners. Some even looked like they had dressed up to go to their office or college, and had changed their minds, but not their clothes. The anonymity of the multitude had provided them cover and a conduit to vent years of pent-up frustration and anger. For some it was all just fun; they were here because they could, or because they had nothing else to do. They broke into shops, tore down traffic lights, vandalized cars and even a couple of bus-stop shelters. When a group of men broke into a shop and cracked a car's headlamp, it inspired the other groups to do the same. A posse of policemen were shuttling back and forth between locations and groups depending on where there was more violence. It was exhausting. Police jeeps would be too slow in such a crowd and we were literally running from one place to another on foot in Mumbai's searing heat.

The mob was now several hundred strong and growing. The policemen, barely a hundred of us, were now being pushed back. Our duty was to protect these people, as well as the property that they seemed so determined to damage. We could have opened fire, but given their numbers, and the mob fury, this might have served to escalate the violence on both sides. Once you open fire, it is hard to stop. The rioters treat that as a sign of their victory, and their violence escalates and spreads. It is an endless downward spiral. We had to do two things: localize their violence and abate their fury.

We closed off several major roads near Minara Masjid, J.J. Hospital and Bhendi Bazaar. I had no idea that things were worsening in the small lane opposite us, Underia Street.

My handheld wireless crackled to life. It was Inspector Bhalerao, who was stationed near Suleiman Chowki at the entrance to Underia Street. 'Zende saheb, things are really bad at Suleiman Chowki. They need urgent help! A mob has attacked the chowki. They are trying to break it. They have already stabbed one constable who tried to defend the chowki. We are unable to evacuate the injured to a hospital. And the mob is not backing down. There are more people in the chowki, and I think *he lok konala nahi sodnar* (these people may not spare anyone). Please do something.'

The Police Control Room also picked up the message and immediately dispatched a wireless van to Suleiman Chowki. It was a large van and could easily accommodate the injured. The van also had fourteen rifle-bearing policemen, including a sub-inspector in it and could provide some security to the chowki staff. I could see the chowki, from where we were at J.J. Junction. But we had been so focused on the mob in front of us on

Mohammed Ali Road that this situation off to one side had gone unnoticed until the wireless message reached us.

The wireless van made its way to the chowki, siren blaring. Underia Street was a narrow road, with shops on either side. It was big enough for a small car to pass through, but a tight fit for a large wireless van. The van entered some 100 feet into the street, avoiding potholes, and stopped close to the chowki's entrance. Five of the armed cops swiftly got out. Three stood guard at the rear entrance of the van, guns at the ready. Two escorted the injured constable as the chowki staff quickly carried him into the van and returned to their posts. At the sight of so many armed policemen and the blaring sirens, the mob was momentarily stunned into inaction. Maybe seeing the injured policeman being taken away cooled tempers. Whatever the reason, they allowed the stabbed constable to be carried into the van. We now had to take him to J.J. Hospital as soon as possible.

The van readied to reverse out on to Maulana Shaukat Ali Road. This was going to be tricky on that narrow street. There was no room for a U-turn. The driver had to reverse out of the street, and continue in reverse for about 200 metres on M.S. Ali Road, avoiding the roadwork in progress there.

As the van's engine revved, the mob regained its battle face. At least a hundred people surrounded the vehicle in a tight circle. The driver dared not move in case he hit someone. Then, a shot rang out. It was not clear who had fired it. It may have been a policeman from the van. No one was hurt, so clearly it was fired in the air, but despite that, it seemed like the last straw, the final shove that pushed the mob over the edge. A collective roar went up from the crowd surrounding the police van.

Deranged with anger, the men picked up whatever they could find—mostly large stones and pipes from the roadworks site on M.S. Ali Road—and began to throw them at the van.

'*Ab tumko nahi chhodega* (We will not let you go)!'

'*Bh**ch**, samajhta kya hai apne aapko* (F*****, who the hell do you think you are)?'

'*Tum logon ko jala daalega* (We will set you on fire)!'

When I came to know of the violence that was spiralling out of control at Suleiman Chowki, I was still at J.J. Junction, and there were several senior officers with me: two deputy commissioners of police and an additional commissioner. Everyone was dumbstruck by the situation and at a complete loss about how to defuse the tension. We could all see the stranded van. We could hear their pleas for help on our wireless radios.

'*Kahitari kara laukar* (Please do something quickly)!'

'*Amhi kai karu, saheb* (What shall we do, sir)?'

'The mob is very big. They are going to burn us alive!'

'Please do something! Help us! Save us!'

But what was the way out of this? If we opened fire to disperse the mob, several people would die, adding more fuel to the fire. It would only ensure that the mob killed all men in some horrific manner, like setting the van on fire. It would lead to a bloodbath. This had never happened in the history of Mumbai. Opening fire was not a solution. We had to save our men. I had to save them!

In that moment, I knew what I had to do. When I get into action mode, I harbour no doubt and focus only on the situation. What I was going to do would seem foolhardy or reckless to some, but at that time it seemed like the only viable solution. And I was aware that I alone could pull it off.

I had worked in that area for several years now and frequently interacted with the people who lived and worked there. I met them near their homes and shops, participated in their events and festivals, and resolved their petty disputes almost every day. In other words, these people knew me not only as a policeman but as a person. They knew how I thought and acted, and they were aware that I did not have any communal bias. In my heart, I knew these people well. I knew that they were angry, but they were not murderers. I felt that their anger should be responded to with trust rather than power. I decided to lead with this trust and stepped forward toward the mob. Alone.

I approached the two or three people who had been barking orders to the rioters.

'*Dekho, yeh theek nahi hai, abhi tabadtop in logon ko roko* (Look, this is wrong, you have to stop these people right now)! Let the policemen in the wireless van go. They have not hurt you. If you hurt them, it will have terrible consequences. Let them go, then do what you want. If you agree, I will go in and get the van out. Alone.'

They were taken aback by the offer. There were brief, hushed discussions between the seven or eight people in charge. Finally, one spoke up. '*Saab, humko aap pe bharosa hai* (Sir, we have faith in you). If you go in alone, with no staff or officers, we will let you bring the van out. You cannot take out your revolver. If anyone fires a bullet, we cannot guarantee what will happen. No one can fire.'

I agreed. '*Maine aaj tak kabhi logon pe goli nahin chalaai* (I have never fired a bullet at people). I will not touch my revolver. Leave the van and the people in it unharmed.'

A couple of the leaders ran ahead towards the mob surrounding the van and told them what was going to happen. There were some arguments, but ultimately it was settled. I moved forward, both my hands raised to show I had no weapons and to pacify the crowd. I have a very loud voice, and I bellowed in a reassuring yet trembling tone, '*Main akela hoon* (I am alone). No guns. I only want you to let the van come out.'

About 150 people marched behind me, as though to escort me, and also to ensure I did not renege on my promise. Every step of those 200 metres seemed to take forever. My heart was thumping hard in my chest, but my mind was clear.

We walked into Underia Street. The mob removed the pipes and stones surrounding the van. I reassured the policemen in the van, who were all trembling like leaves.

'*Ghabru naka. Tumhala kahi nahi honar.* (Don't be scared. You will not be harmed.) Put your guns down.' I assured the policemen repeatedly.

I was their boss. Like the people in the area, I had earned their trust too; and what they had seen in the last couple of minutes gave them some confidence. They lowered their guns.

There was no room to turn the van in that narrow lane, so the driver started reversing out. Wireless van drivers are usually experts, but this man was under tremendous pressure, and he could barely see the potholed road. He backed up the van into a large pothole, and the van got stuck! Incredibly, the same crowd that had threatened to burn the van now surged forward and collectively lifted the van and the people in it out of the pothole. It was an incredible sight to behold. We had nearly accomplished our mission.

I felt like a batsman who had scored ninety-nine runs. A lot was done, but I still had to be careful while getting the last run to reach a hundred. The van inched backwards, and finally got out of the lane, and navigated down M.S. Ali Road to J.J. Junction. In the excitement of making the final turn on to Mohammed Ali Road, the van's driver lost control and swerved too fast. The van keeled over and fell on one side. But the policemen in it were all safe and very grateful. 'Saheb, you saved our lives today. We will forever be grateful to you.'

Our senior officers were just dumbstruck by what they had just witnessed. My brain and body were suffused with adrenaline, and whatever hormone convinces you that you are doing the right thing, unmindful of any personal harm. It was a great moment for me, but there was no time for any celebration.

Rioting broke out in several areas across Dongri and Pydhonie. Trouble started in the Chaar Nal area. We rushed there. Then, things flared up in the BIT Chawl area. We rushed there. This was repeated in several areas. We were constantly rushing between severely troubled spots. The mobs broke into shops, ransacked them, and burnt or broke the goods and wares inside. When all other means to stop them failed, we opened fire in some areas.

Over the next thirty hours, seventeen rioters fell to police bullets. The rioting which started on the morning of 7 December only abated by the evening of 8 December. Going home, sleeping or bathing were out of the question for us policemen during this time. We were beyond exhausted, but rest was still a distant dream.

We stabilized the area over the next two days. On 11 December, we organized a meeting of the Peace Committee of the Pydhonie and Dongri areas. Their leaders accepted that the police was not to blame for the deaths of the seventeen people.

'They were rioters and were wrong. You punished them. That was the right thing to do. We have no problem with that. We will support you in maintaining peace,' they told us.

Then, we organized a meeting of 300–400 local leaders in Dongri. They also promised to maintain peace. But we were not done.

Later that day, a rumour started that some small mosques were issuing a 'cautionary warning' that 'no one should go near Dongri; Hindu goons are waiting there. They say "Ram Ram", and if you don't respond, they stab you'.

We knew this was not true. No such incident had been reported. But the people in the area were not going to take the word of the police over that of their local religious leaders and rumour-mongers. We needed to convince the local leaders first. I summoned all the elected municipal corporators of those areas and took them with me to the so-called affected areas.

'*Khabar hai idhar stabbing hua hai* (We received news there's been a stabbing here). Show me who was stabbed and where,' I asked the people in one of these streets.

'*Idhar toh aisa kuchh nahin hai, sahab. Baju wali gali me hua rahenga* (Nothing happened here, sir. Maybe it was the next street),' the person said.

We went there and asked the same question. Still nothing. In this way, we assured the corporators that the rumours were unfounded. They were convinced. We then made them announce over the PA systems of the same cautioning masjids that these were just rumours; that all was well, and people should maintain peace and harmony. Calm was restored to the city. A calm before a much bigger storm ...

3

THE RISE AND ARREST OF CHARLES SOBHRAJ

Shashi Raut ordered his third Thums Up—three more than he had drunk in the last thirteen years. The sugar kept him alert as he waited. This was already his second evening of waiting at Goa's famous O'Coqueiro Bar & Restaurant, located in Porvorim, just off the Mumbai–Goa highway.

Shashi's friends sat inside the bar with their beers. O'Coqueiro's famous chicken cafreal went wonderfully with it. They were all trying to enjoy the India–Pakistan hockey match on the TV, but their attention was routinely diverted by the boisterous wedding party in progress. Loud, merry and very Goan, the generous hosts were welcoming of anyone who wanted to join the evening's revelry. At 11 p.m., the party was just getting started.

Shashi was not interested in any of this. Sitting at the table near the entrance of the bar, he kept an eye on every car that stopped at the entrance of O'Coqueiro. Thanks to the party, there were not too many more visitors today. He briefly scanned every face; he knew he would not need to look too closely. Even though he had last seen the man he sought nearly ten years ago, he knew that he would recognize him immediately.

For the last five days, Shashi had put his entire life on hold, his sole purpose being to hunt down this one man. He had gone to great lengths—even giving up his name—for this singular quest. He had left his home in Mumbai; his wife and three children had only a vague idea of his whereabouts. Since his quarry had killed more than twenty people already and was known to carry a gun in his pocket, there was no telling if they would ever see him again. But Shashi had long stopped thinking about that. He was living at the Taj Hermitage, Goa's best hotel, located in Sinquerim, that was clearly beyond his means, pretending to be someone he was not, just so he could put this man away forever. Was there anything he would stop at to accomplish his mission, he wondered. All because he knew—no, he *believed*—that if anyone could find this man and prevent another string of deaths, it was he, Shashi Raut.

The man was a robber, fraudster, confidence trickster, and strangler, killer and immolator of men and women across countries. Thanks to an Interpol Red corner notice, the police in at least one hundred countries were looking for him. His last string of victims was overland Western hippie travellers in Thailand and Nepal. Goa had plenty of those, and would have been the perfect base for him. He might have been hunting already.

*

Gurmukh Charles Sobhraj was born in war-torn Saigon (now Ho Chi Minh City), Vietnam. His father, Hotchand Sobhraj, was an influential and successful Indian-origin businessman based there. Charles's Vietnamese mother, Noi, was a survivor. She had escaped her abjectly poor childhood and started working as an assistant in Hotchand's tailoring shop, and became the mother of his two children. When her relationship with Hotchand was looking unlikely to result in marriage, she married a French armyman, Jacques Roussel, who had been forced out of his desk job to fight the Viet Minh on the ground. When Jacques could not bear the fighting any longer, he and Noi moved back to France. Charles reluctantly moved with them. Since Vietnam had been a French colony, in those days, it was possible for Sobhraj to get French citizenship. However, he turned to crime very early in life, and it took persistent efforts by his stepfather to get him this passport.

Sobhraj had a troubled childhood, struggling to find a stable home and a sense of belonging. Starting as a street hustler, he graduated to gambling, theft and stealing cars. He progressively built up his reputation as a conman, fraudster, thief, armed robber, and of course a killer. His biographers, Richard Neville and Julie Clarke, describe Charles as 'an incorrigible criminal whose career [sent] the world's press into paroxysms of grisly prose'.[3]

The man had admitted to killing at least a dozen people, although he also recanted that confession.[4] Interpol's Red notice meant that all of its hundred-plus member nations were required to arrest Sobhraj whether or not he was wanted in their country.

'The first killing he confessed to, according to his biographers, was a Pakistani taxi driver in 1972. But it is in Thailand where his alleged murder spree ramped up.' He had killed the taxi driver, put his corpse in the car's boot and kept driving. Later, when the stench became too overwhelming, he threw the dead man in a stream that they were passing.

Reuters reported that he was also wanted for the murder of six bikini-clad women in Pattaya, Thailand, in 1975.[5]

In October 1975, he befriended and killed American citizen Teresa Knowlton, who was headed to a Buddhist

---

3 'The Serpent: Who were the real life victims of Charles Sobhraj?' *Cosmopolitan*, 7 February 2021, https://www.cosmopolitan.com/uk/reports/a35176308/serpent-charles-sobhraj-victims/

4 Julia Hollingsworth and Adam Renton, 'From diplomat to detective, this man helped bring Asia's notorious "Serpent" killer to justice', CNN, 14 March 2021, https://edition.cnn.com/2021/03/13/asia/serpent-bikini-killer-sobhraj-intl-hnk-dst/index.html

5 'Who is the "bikini killer" Charles Sobhraj?', Reuters, 21 December 2022, https://www.reuters.com/world/asia-pacific/who-is-bikini-killer-charles-sobhraj-2022-12-21/

monastery.[6] For a few hundred dollars' worth of possessions, Sobhraj drugged her, and when she was unconscious, changed her into a bikini and then drowned her. Her body was found in the Gulf of Thailand, earning Sobhraj the moniker 'Bikini Killer'.

In 1976, two charred bodies were found near Ayutthaya in Thailand. They were later identified as a Dutch couple, Henricus Bintanja and Cornelia Hemker. Charles Sobhraj was convicted in a Thai court of having befriended, drugged, killed and burned this couple.

In October 1975, Sobhraj is reported to have also killed a Turkish man, Vitali 'Ved' Hakim, whose charred body was found in some fields in the vicinity of the gem mines of Chanthaburi. A few days later he killed Ved's friend, Stephanie Barry, who had tried to investigate his death.[7]

The same year, he visited Nepal, where he killed a Canadian woman, Connie Jo Bronzich, and her American friend, Laurent Carriere. He was convicted of these murders decades later, and served nineteen years in a Nepal jail. In both convictions, diligent investigations conducted by former Dutch diplomat Hermann Knippenberg are said to have helped significantly.

---

6 'Who Was Teresa Knowlton, the First Known Victim of "The Serpent's" Charles Sobhraj?', *Women's Health*, 2 April 2021.

7 *On the Trail of the Serpent*, Richard Neville and Julie Clark, Penguin Books, 2021.

During this period, he also visited India, and he was reported to have killed Israeli scholar Avoni Jacob and also Frenchman Jean-Luc Solomon.[8]

He liked to cast his net wide and befriend many people. Many of them saw him in possession of several passports. Possibly, he had murdered some or all of the passport owners. He was known to doctor the passports, and travel around the world using them. He is said to have killed his own accomplice, Ajay Chowdhry, in Malaysia.[9]

In 1976, he used one such stolen passport and escaped from Thailand to India.

In India, he was wanted for several crimes by then, but he managed to stay ahead of the police. That was until desperation and an alert hotel manager did him in.

Raut and Sobhraj's connection went back a long time—sixteen years to be precise. It began when Charles first appeared in Indian newspaper headlines in 1970.

*

---

8 'The Serpent: Who were the real life victims of Charles Sobhraj?', *Cosmopolitan*, 7 February 2021, https://www.cosmopolitan.com/uk/reports/a35176308/serpent-charles-sobhraj-victims/

9 Andrew Anthony, 'Speaking with the Serpent: my encounters with serial killer Charles Sobhraj', *The Guardian*, 27 December 2020, https://www.theguardian.com/tv-and-radio/2020/dec/27/speaking-with-the-serpent-my-encounters-with-serial-killer-charles-sobhraj

The Ashok was a gem in the state-owned Indian Tourism Development Corporation's hospitality necklace. Spread over nearly a hundred acres in New Delhi's Chanakyapuri, The Ashok was famous for its palatial rooms and suites, sprawling lobbies and corridors, opulent restaurants and attentive service-staff. It evoked the lifestyles of the rajahs of India and was a magnet for international tourists—especially those with fat wallets and a lot of prestige to throw around. Naturally, shopping was another highlight of the hotel. Several shops sold carpets, silks, handicrafts of exquisite quality, and of course, jewellery. The best-cut gemstones and ornately crafted ornaments dazzled in brightly lit shop windows. The region's top merchants were happy to pay the cost of owning a shop in The Ashok. It was like a mediaeval Samarkand in the middle of Delhi. Shoppers thronged these stores, except the truly rich and aristocratic ones who would not deign to step into a shop.

So, one day in 1970, when the owner of a famous jewellery shop was asked to send some exquisite necklaces to a suite in the hotel, he was not surprised. The caller claimed to be a prince, and wanted to buy some jewellery for his new fiancée. The shop-owner sent his trusted manager, who spoke fluent English, with two velvet-lined suitcases, custom-built for just such a purpose. Each suitcase held six necklaces. None were the shop's top-of-the-line stuff. The seller wanted to gauge how rich this prince really was.

The manager's first impression of the prince must have been very positive. He looked unusually strong for a man who was much less than six feet tall. He was dressed in a cream-coloured silk suit, and his azure silk shirt was unbuttoned to reveal a bare and muscular chest. In the fashion of celebrities, he wore sunglasses even indoors—not very dark ones, just enough to shade his eyes. He cursorily responded to the manager's deep bow with the barest of nods. Wordlessly, he spun around, and walked into the room, and settled into a plush chair. The manager took this as a sign of being invited in, and sat on the edge of a chair opposite the prince; in the chair next to him sat a woman who the manager recognized as the cabaret dancer from the hotel's Middle-East-themed restaurant. In today's parlance, it looked like she had found herself an ultra-rich sugar daddy. The manager, whose name was Malhotra, politely bowed to her and murmured a 'hello ma'am' before settling down to his task.

He carefully, hands slightly trembling, presented each necklace, keeping up a running commentary about the quality of the stones, their origin, craftsmanship and anything else he could think of to fill the stately silence. The prince nodded assent to two of the first three pieces. This was going well. The manager rewarded himself by pouring out a glass of water from the jug in front of him and drained the glass in one large gulp.

Ten minutes later, he was out like a light. Then, he was tied firmly to his chair, blindfolded and gagged.

The 'prince' knew his job. He knew good jewellery, and he also knew how to tie and drug people. In twenty minutes, he and his lady companion had packed their bags, including the necklaces, called a hotel taxi, and sped off towards the airport.

After waiting more than ninety minutes for his manager to return from the prince's suite, the jewellery shop owner grew anxious. He called the hotel suite in question, but there was no response. That was strange. The manager had specific instructions to always answer the phone in such circumstances, while keeping the goods squarely in his sight. The owner decided to investigate for himself and convinced a hotel security staff member to accompany him. When their knocks went unanswered, they used the hotel's master key. The manager, who was still in his chair, did not turn around when they entered, nor when they called his name. The necklaces were nowhere to be seen; nor were the supposed occupants of the palatial suite.

The security staff called in more colleagues, and they hurriedly scanned the wardrobes and drawers in the suite. The 'prince' had left a passport behind, one of several he had doctored, as revealed later. The name on it read 'Charles Sobhraj'. The door attendant revealed that the handsome 'prince' and his beautiful 'fiancée' were headed to the airport. Things moved quickly after that. The hotel management was alerted, and they immediately called the police. Based on a police notification, the airport sound system requested Mr Charles Sobhraj to report to the airlines counter. Charles knew they were onto him. Making an excuse to his lady companion that he was going to the restroom, he quietly disappeared, both from Delhi and her life.

The next day, Charles Sobhraj's name headlined the crime pages. Although the necklaces and dancer returned to the hotel, the audacity of the operation and the obvious swagger of the handsome thief made for great reading. This incident stayed in public memory for a long time.

Late in 1970, he got together a gang of seven or eight accomplices he had worked with before, whom he could trust. These men stole four expensive cars from Iran, gathered a few revolvers, pistols, rifles and a couple of grenades, and began their journey by road to the capital of India.

The Afghan and Persian invaders of the seventeenth and eighteenth centuries had met their fiercest opposition from the Marathas. Unbeknownst to Sobhraj and his gang, in 1970 too, one Maratha soldier was readying to do battle with him.

*

Mumbai-based Ajay Modi was the spoilt son of well-off Gujarati parents. Barely out of his teens in 1971, no indulgence was too much for him. Smoking expensive cigarettes, chillums of charas and ganja; binge-drinking expensive Scotch and visiting sex-workers were all routine. Ajay was always on the lookout for the next high. And in June, that high came from crime. He started small and at home—he stole 300 grams of gold jewellery (worth over USD 20,000 at the time of writing this book) from his mother's cupboard and ran away.

Ajay's parents were more concerned about the disappearance of their dear son than the loss of the jewellery and did everything they could to locate him. When all their personal attempts failed, they approached the local police station at Gamdevi in south Mumbai.

As fate would have it, the case was assigned to me. Within a few days, we traced Ajay to a lodge in the Paltan Road area. He was holed up there with a sex worker. We arrested him, recovered most of the jewellery and sent the case for prosecution. He was easily convicted. But seeing their beloved son in handcuffs as a convicted criminal melted his parents' hearts. They beseeched me to avoid sending their son to jail. As a parent, I empathized with them. Besides, the penal system of India allowed for new offenders to be treated mildly to ensure that they did not become hardened criminals, as many are wont to become after serving jail-time.

I made the required representation to the police prosecutor, who acceded to our request. Ajay was not sent to prison. Instead, he was set free on a two-year bond, dependent on his good behaviour. Delighted with the outcome, the Modis brought Ajay to meet me. He was a slightly built youth of about twenty, around five foot five inches tall, and sported a thin moustache. I noticed how his eyes had a slightly glazed expression—probably from drug use. Cowed down by his recent tryst with the law, Ajay bowed deeply with folded hands,

'Jai Shri Krishna, sir. Thank you very much for your help, sir,' he greeted me in fluent English.

I asked them to sit down.

'Ajay this was your first offence,' I said. 'And you are a fine young man with a bright future. So, the court has granted our request this time. Your parents love you so much. I understand that as a young man, you want to have fun, so you do all these wild things. It is natural, but you must be careful to not cross the fine line between having fun and committing a crime. If you don't stop now, you will ruin your life as well as that of your parents. Is that what you want?'

'No, sir. I understand what you mean. I will mend my ways. I have talked to my parents already. I am going to start working for the family business. That will keep me occupied. Once I succeed in making money, I will not need any other high.'

Ajay seemed to have thought this through.

'That's wonderful, Ajay. Hope we don't have to meet like this again,' I replied.

'I promise you, sir. This will not happen again.'

'But remember to call me for your wedding,' I added, in a lighter vein.

Visibly blushing, Ajay smiled and said, 'Of course, sir.' We had a good laugh.

However, highs are addictive. Ajay was now hooked on crime. After this incident, he did become involved in the family business, but secretly craved another high, and this time, in the form of a good heist.

In those days, Girgaon Chowpatty after dark was a dirty, dingy place that most decent folks avoided. It was only visited by those seeking Mumbai's darker pleasures. One such evening in October 1971, Ajay Modi was walking on the Chowpatty, eyes and ears peeled for any action. It was just after dusk; the sea looked ink blue. He avoided the sev puri and pani puri stalls near Anand Milk shop, where families thronged, choosing instead to walk on the unlit, less-crowded, seedy part of the beach. Masseurs were hawking on-the-spot massages. The so-called 'happy endings', which were locally known as 'paani nikaalna', were double charge. He had occasionally bought dope from a couple of these masseurs, but that's not what he wanted this evening. He walked past couples eagerly waiting for the sun to sink further down. In the midst of it all, his attention was inexorably drawn to a man watching the gently incoming tide, although he seemed equally alert to his surroundings. The man was not much taller than Ajay but exuded great strength. The way in which he lifted his hand to his lips to take a deep drag from his cigarette had a swagger that immediately attracted Ajay. The darkness and the shades he wore hid the angle of his gaze, but he seemed to acknowledge Ajay's presence with a gentle nod. Ajay could not believe it. This man was clearly not Indian, and as far as Ajay was concerned, not even from the same planet. Something about him drew Ajay like a compass to the magnetic north. It was as though he held the ticket to the world Ajay wanted to escape to. If only he could get to know him ...

Ajay hesitatingly approached this man and struck up a conversation. The exotic stranger responded with an even more exotic and silken accent. From close quarters, Ajay noticed he had rather high cheekbones, and his complexion even in the dark appeared east Asian. His calm manner suggested that he was used to having this magnetic effect on people.

Ajay made up his mind to impress this man, and to somehow get close to him.

After talking with him for a few minutes, Ajay felt this man probably did not live within the rules and mores of common society. He considered himself above these.

Ajay was taken aback. But the possibility that this man was actually a criminal sent a bolt of excitement through Ajay's body. Could he really be speaking to an international crime-lord? He decided to push his luck; opportunity only knocks once.

Ajay subtly conveyed to the stranger that he too was not afraid of flouting the law. It worked, and the stranger revealed his cards. He asked Ajay if he was familiar with the Air India office in the Fort area and if he could make a detailed plan to rob that office. In those days, there were few airlines operating international flights to India, ticket prices were quite high, and many booked seats by paying cash. So looting the Air India office would be quite lucrative.

Although the task seemed nearly impossible to Ajay, he was excited at the prospect of this big heist and committed to make a detailed plan in just a few days. They agreed to meet soon at the Taj Mahal Hotel in Colaba, where the stranger told him he was staying. Ajay was told to ask for Mr Charles Sobhraj.

Ajay had heard the name in the news; Sobhraj had carried out that nearly successful and completely audacious heist at New Delhi's The Ashok. Ajay felt like his life's trajectory was taking an upward turn, and he had finally found a mentor and purpose.

Ajay put his heart into the project. The Air India ticketing office was opposite the University of Mumbai. During the day time, Ajay studied it closely. He visited the office a few times on the pretext of inquiring about buying, changing and cancelling tickets, and observed how cash was handled. He entered and exited the building several times from different doors, used the stairs above and below. He studied the office access from the street and the roof. As he waited, he observed how the staff moved cash to and from the safes.

The office was located in the very busy Fort area, with the bustling M.G. Road on one side and smaller lanes on the other. He mapped the flow and volume of foot and vehicular traffic on all these roads. He spoke to some of the shopkeepers, careful not to get so familiar that they would remember him. He understood what drove the traffic volumes during the day.

After hours, he drew up a detailed plan of how the heist would be executed—when they would do it, which road they would enter from, where they would park for a quick getaway, where could a back-up car be parked in advance, where would stakeouts be placed, who would demand the money, who would fill the sacks, how many people would carry them out to the cars, and how they would all get away before any alarms were raised.

Two days later, he walked Charles through his detailed plan and knocked the socks off his newfound mentor. Charles invited Ajay to meet the rest of his gang in Delhi. Ajay was now truly flying.

Ajay rushed home and packed a suitcase for his departure, which would be in two days. 'Home' was now a small room in a hostel; his parents had got wind of his return to the world of crime and, to avoid any further untoward incidents in the house, had booted him out.

In Delhi, Sobhraj stayed at the Taj, but he put the others in smaller hotels in the Paharganj area, which even hosts budget backpackers from all parts of the world. The staff there didn't ask too many questions. Ajay shared a room with one of the other members of Sobhraj's gang. Each of the Afghan and Iranian men carried some scars of past adventures and at least two weapons. They all gathered in Ajay's hotel room to fine-tune their plan and that's when he saw their arsenal of weapons—three pistols, four revolvers, two handguns, and two hand-grenades.

The dhokla–fafda eating Gujarati boy from Mumbai had only read about such weapons. His initial excitement soon turned to terror. He forced himself to sit through the planning session. Visions of how these hardened mercenaries might unleash terror and violence in this city filled him with fear—revulsion, even. He wanted out. A life of serious crime was clearly not what Ajay had imagined it would be.

Late at night, long after the group had dispersed and his roommate had gone to sleep, Ajay quietly snuck out of the hotel room. His business mind told him that these high-grade revolvers would fetch a good price in Mumbai, and he stole two. His heart racing with the fear of being caught, Ajay made his way to the bus stand, and stayed on the move till he reached his dingy hostel room in Mumbai.

Now he had to stay off Sobhraj's radar, and somehow make a living. Encashing his only legit work experience, he started a small roadside stall that sold cigarettes in Girgaon, near Harkisandas Narottamdas Hospital. He managed to eke out a living, and quickly found a rich looking guy who seemed like a good customer for an imported revolver. Ajay's quoted price of five thousand rupees was accepted immediately, and the trade was completed within minutes. Ajay decided to charge more for the next one.

In a couple of days, an affluent looking young man approached him, quaking with nervous excitement. He had heard on the grapevine that Ajay had a gun to sell.

Both were nervous about making this surreptitious deal. Neither drove a hard bargain, and they quickly agreed on a price. The only problem was that the buyer did not know how to use a gun. He asked Ajay for a tutorial. Now came the real problem—Ajay didn't know either. But he did not let on. He agreed to teach the buyer how to use a gun that evening. A rendezvous was set at the S.K. Patil Udyan on the Marine Lines road—a small, poorly lit park, frequented by elderly morning walkers and little children with their ayahs (nannies), which was mostly empty after sunset.

They walked under the dim street lights towards the park. The evening traffic rush on Queen's Road was over now, and only an occasional black-and-yellow Premier Padmini taxi whizzed past. A double-decker BEST bus, serving route 122, crossed them in the opposite direction, and Ajay momentarily relived the joyrides he had taken in the front seat, the wind blowing in his hair. He had come a long way.

Ajay and his buyer stood between two slides shaped to look like cartoon animals. Ajay wanted to make this quick. It must have been an amusing sight. One proud owner of a newly acquired lethal weapon, being taught how to use it by an equally clueless teacher. It had a tragic ending. No one had told Ajay that guns have safety catches that can prevent accidental firing. The one in his gun was not locked.

In his nervousness, Ajay squeezed the trigger too tightly. The gun fired; the bullet struck the buyer square in the chest. He collapsed instantly. Terror-struck at what he had done, Ajay did what he did best—he ran. What could he do now? Had he just killed a guy? He really did not want to. But who would believe him? Who would help him? Sobhraj? No way. Sobhraj would probably kill him. He needed someone who could counter Sobhraj. Yes! He knew the cop who had helped him just a few months before. He sprinted towards Gamdevi police station.

I was on night duty and sitting in my office. Ajay ran up to me, and pointed the revolver at my face. His words came out in a torrent.

'Sahab! Sahab! I didn't mean to kill him! Save me, save me!'

Taken aback, I tried to talk him down.

'Ajay! What are you doing here? And what is this gun? What are you talking about? First, first put the gun down,' I said.

He placed it on the edge of my desk. I used a handkerchief to move it to one side. It was loaded. Ajay had obviously shot someone. We might have a life to save. I sat him down, heard his failed gun-trade story briefly, and dispatched an officer to check on the victim. We learnt soon that a passing samaritan had taken the injured man to a hospital. He was safe. But Ajay's troubles may have only just begun.

'Ajay, who gave you the gun?' I asked him sternly.

'I stole it. From Charles Sobhraj.'

Ajay paused to see my reaction. I had so many questions.

'What? Sobhraj? That fake prince? What are you doing with him?'

'I will tell you the whole story, and also help you to catch him,' Ajay said. He had calmed down with the knowledge of the power his information might give him.

He talked me through the complete details of the Air India robbery plan, the gang members, the weapons they had. As per their original schedule, the heist was planned in about four days. If they were going ahead with the plan, they would now be in my city—professional thieves armed to the teeth with some serious firepower and a clear intent to use it in broad daylight. I had to stop them.

Ajay was a convicted criminal and there was no reason to trust him. Worse, his entire story about Sobhraj may have been a con to distract us from another crime that was planned or already committed. As a cop though, I could not ignore this lead. That's not how we roll. We prepared for the hunt.

Sobhraj had a preference for the Taj chain of hotels, so that was a starting point. We started staking out the lanes near the hotel. There were always four men in a black-and-yellow taxi—Ajay, the driver, and two men to veil Ajay. Each evening, they would wait discreetly at different spots from where the entrance to the Taj Mahal Hotel could be seen. I stood a short distance away, so that Ajay could signal if he spotted Sobhraj, and we could spring upon him without delay. Given that his chief planner had escaped, we were sure Sobhraj had abandoned his plans. But we underestimated his confidence.

On the third evening of the stakeout, 11 November 1971, as I stood outside the La Patisserie cake shop at the Taj, casually snacking on a twenty-paise packet of kharasing (salted peanuts), Ajay gave the signal. My first instinct was to freeze mid-bite, but there was no time for that. I spun around and started walking, fast enough but not too much so. Ten steps ahead of me was a man in a white suit. He was not tall, but he exuded strength and agility. He casually bent forward to light a cigarette, and almost came to a halt. I ran the short distance between us and grabbed him from behind. Two more officers joined in, and then a couple more joined from the side lane. A taxi drove past us, picking up pace. Sobhraj's eyes lingered on it, but he did not resist, nor did he say a word.

The next day's newspaper headlines proudly proclaimed, 'One more feather in Mumbai Police's cap'. It was a proud day for us.

We also got extra brownie points for apprehending a man wanted by the Delhi Police; there was no pending case against Sobhraj in Mumbai. The Delhi Police came down post-haste and shipped him off. And just as quickly, Charles slipped from their grasp.

In 1971, India and Pakistan were on the verge of war over what would become Bangladesh. Each evening, there was a blackout in Delhi to escape detection by enemy planes flying overhead. Sobhraj feigned appendectomy pain and had himself checked into a hospital. Under cover of the blackout, he visited the bathroom, opened a window, climbed down a pipe, and was gone. Out of Delhi, out of India, and into Indian newspapers' headlines once again.

Sobhraj seemed to realize that big heists with large teams were not his thing. He decided to stick to his limited, reptilian strengths of trickery and slipperiness, and rob individuals or small groups, even if the pickings might be slimmer than a big heist—sort of quantity over quality.

After this, Sobhraj went on a killing spree. He is reputed to have killed at least twenty people across Thailand, India and Nepal during this period—drugging, drowning, knifing, burning and burying them.[10] He would charm his victims, win their trust, and proceed with his plans.

During his next trip to India in 1976, he chanced upon an unexpectedly low-hanging target. Forty university students from France were visiting Delhi that summer. Like other Westerners 300 years before, they were completely unprepared for the desert-like temperatures of Delhi's summer, combined with its hot 'lu' or summer breeze. Chilled water in their thermos-flask bottles provided gentle respite as they tried to take in

---

10 'Timeline: Case of Charles Sobhraj—"Bikini Killer", "Serpent"', Al Jazeera, 23 December 2022, https://www.aljazeera.com/news/2022/12/23/timeline-case-of-charles-sobhraj-bikini-killer-serpent

the sights across the city. At the Qutub Minar, they were unexpectedly greeted by a French-speaking man.

The man looked vaguely east Asian, and was clearly a foreigner to India, just like them. He looked older than them, and more experienced in the ways of travelling in these tropical lands. His simple overture in their native tongue was a soothing caress to these heat-harried, homesick boys.

The man immediately sensed their biggest problem—insufficient safe drinking water that would give some respite from the Delhi heat. In those days, bottled water like Evian and Bisleri was not easily available, and the filtered water available at local hotels was often of dubious quality.

The kind stranger told them to stay away from the bottles of filtered water that they were carrying around, and offered to drop off a few bottles of imported bottled water of a brand they could trust. The man sounded like a saviour.

True to his word, post lunch, when the boys got back to their dormitory, they found that the kind stranger had dropped off thirty bottles of a good quality bottled drinking water. They gratefully downed it. The tired youngsters were fast asleep within minutes. Thanks to the generously administered sedative in their water bottles, they stayed asleep—even when the kind stranger slipped into their room and started helping himself to their money, cameras, watches, etc. He knew he had ample time; the boys would not wake up from their drug-laced water till the following morning.

So, he was terribly inconvenienced when there was a tap on his shoulder. He turned around. It did not make sense. What was a cop doing here at this time?

'Saala, aren't you ashamed, stealing from boys like this?' the policeman delivered this reprimand with a side of a resounding slap. 'You think Delhi Police is sleeping?'

There were two more policemen between him and the only door to the room, so running away was not an option.

'Search him,' ordered the inspector. His own name-badge read Narendranath Tuli. The manager of the boys' hotel had sensed a rat when this east Asian–looking, French-speaking stranger got too friendly with his guests, and had proceeded to call the police.

They searched his pockets and found a wallet with currency, and a couple of passports of different countries. They all had the photograph of the same man: Charles Sobhraj.

4

THE SENSATIONAL FALL OF THE SERPENT

On 16 March 1986, David Hall, an international drug dealer and criminal accomplice of Charles Sobhraj, drove into Delhi's high security Tihar Jail complex with boxes of sweets, supposedly for Sobhraj's birthday party. They were distributed liberally among the jail staff.

Sobhraj had now spent a decade in Tihar; they all trusted him and were happy to participate in the celebrations. Within a few minutes of eating the goodies, each one of them succumbed to the strong sedative the sweets were laced with. With literally no jail staff to challenge them, Charles Sobhraj and David Hall drove out to freedom in a car. Fifteen other prisoners also escaped with them, in two other cars.

'Charles Sobhraj's daring escape from Tihar Jail' screamed the next morning's newspapers, highlighting not only the audacity of the criminal minds, but the utter credulity of the policemen in one of India's highest security prisons.

We may never know the whole truth of what exactly happened in Tihar the previous day; so many versions have been offered. But the main contours seem to be these: during his ten years in Tihar, Sobhraj established very good relationships with the jail staff. He enjoyed 'television and gourmet food'.[11] His accomplices were able to supply him with gifts and money to live a privileged life, even in prison. His escape was but a product of this privilege and misplaced trust on the part of his jailers. They should have known better.

The infamous escape had several elements that Sobhraj was known for: the use of sedatives that are potent enough to kill, winning over people around him, and the sheer audacity of his plans. He had given policemen the slip not only in Delhi, but in several other cities over the world. There was no reason for anyone to trust him.

As the person who had arrested him, I found this news difficult to wrap my head around. As a trained policeman, there were several questions that immediately came to my mind. Did the jail staff not know when Sobhraj's birthday was? How could they accept food from a murderer whose main MO was powerful drugs? How

---

11 Himanshi Dahiya, '*The "Bikini Killer" Who Fled Tihar: Charles Sobhraj's India Connection*', The Quint, 22 December 2022.

could so many jailers in India's most secure prison get so intoxicated that they could not stop their most dangerous inmate from walking out?

My own experience showed that Sobhraj had developed an unusual amount of ruthless disregard for other people's lives. He was quite content to collaborate with people while they served his purpose, and coolly dispose of them when he was done. Self-preservation was one of his strongest characteristics.

*

In 1971, the Taj and the Oberoi were the top names in five-star luxury in Mumbai. Popular among affluent visitors and tourists to India, they were also the preferred hunting ground for Sobhraj, who preferred these international travellers.

Bob Thomas, the security chief of the Taj Mahal Hotel in Colaba at the time, was my acquaintance. Since I was handling Sobhraj's case, I met with Bob, showed him a picture of Sobhraj, and told him to stay alert for the criminal. Bob seemed to know Sobhraj even better than me.

'Don't worry, Zende. I know this man well. He and I studied karate together some years ago in Japan. We appeared for our black-belt exams together. He is very quick and sharp, but has no moral qualms. He will do whatever it takes to have his way. I am not surprised that he is a criminal. My staff and I will be glad to help you.'

Barely two months later, a French couple staying at the hotel had lunch with another foreign couple staying there, and became quite ill after. They passed out in their hotel beds. When they regained consciousness, all their valuables, including money, electronics and passports had been stolen. Recognizing Sobhraj's MO, I showed the couple his photograph, and they immediately confirmed it was the man they had lunched with. Their blood tests revealed the presence of a powerful sedative.

Shocked that Sobhraj had already struck under his watch, Bob promised to be even more vigilant. He soon got another opportunity.

Late one afternoon, while on duty at the hotel's security desk, Bob saw Sobhraj enjoying afternoon tea at the Shamiana coffee shop with a blonde girl. Smartly dressed, Sobhraj looked different from the man whom Bob had only seen in a loose white karate dogi.

Bob cloaked his racing pulse with a calm walk back to his desk and, keeping one eye on Sobhraj, proceeded to place a call to me at my Colaba police station office. That moment of distraction, while Bob dialled my number, was all Sobhraj needed. By the time Bob looked up from the phone, Sobhraj and the girl were gone. Guessing they had left the hotel in a taxi, Bob rushed to the hotel's front gate that was very close to the Shamiana. He noticed that the tall, turbaned guard at the main gate had also disappeared.

Confused, he came back to his desk to work out what may have happened. By the time I got there with my team,

Bob had a news update. The hotel guard had called him from Churchgate's Ritz hotel. Sobhraj was there.

The guard had shown remarkable presence of mind and grit when Sobhraj and the girl had rushed out of the Taj, shoved aside a couple about to enter a waiting taxi, and zoomed off. The guard had been surprised at this behaviour by a foreign-looking couple. Perhaps he also recognized Sobhraj from the picture that Bob had circulated. Whatever the reason, the guard jumped into the very next taxi and followed Sobhraj.

We rushed to the Ritz; Sobhraj had been staying there. By the time we reached, he managed to check out and was just boarding a taxi as we pulled in close to the hotel. Seeing the police jeep, he abandoned his belongings and bolted on foot. It was the evening rush hour at Churchgate station, and he blended into the crowd.

We arrested the girl, who was glad to have escaped from Sobhraj's clutches. From his luggage in the taxi, we recovered quite a stash. There were stolen passports that confirmed his identity as Charles Sobhraj. We also recovered currency notes of various countries, and some cleverly disguised ammunition. There were automatic pistols concealed within cans of Yardley talcum powder. The cans' flat design concealed the weapon well. A box of chocolates contained bullets, each wrapped individually in chocolate wrappers.

Sobhraj had given us the slip, but not for long. By 1976, he was back to Delhi, where Narendranath Tuli arrested him.

In October 1977, Sobhraj was being tried for various crimes in India. I was called as a witness. Since my wife, Vijaya, had never been to Delhi before, she too came along at our personal expense. We reached Tis Hazari Court about an hour before my scheduled time of appearance. We were waiting outside the courthouse, observing the goings-on at that bureaucratic-looking cinder block. It was public knowledge that the international 'Bikini Killer' would be appearing that day and that had attracted quite a crowd. Soon, we heard the sirens of an approaching police van. It was preceded by a jeep, also with sirens blaring. Both vehicles stopped directly before the courthouse entrance. Two armed policemen jumped out of the jeep and trotted towards the rear entrance to the van. Only then, Inspector Tuli and one sub-inspector jumped out. They were followed by a strong-looking man of average height, wearing a crisp white shirt and pants. He wore handcuffs, and the chains around his wrists and ankles were firmly held by a cop each.

The man in chains seemed to quietly enjoy the attention and walked at a relaxed pace towards the courthouse. I was amazed that a man of his physical stature needed so much security, and I couldn't resist making that observation.

'*Ek aadmi ke liye itna policewallah* (So many cops for one man)?'

'*Oye, janta hai kya woh kaun hai* (Do you know who he is)? He has killed over forty people,' said one local bystander Dilliwala.

'Of course I know, he is Charles Sobhraj. I arrested him,' I shot back.

'Looks like you are a madman,' he muttered under his breath, and hurried off with his friends towards the courthouse.

Since I was to stand witness, I too proceeded in the same direction. Vijaya stayed back in the yard, preferring it to the packed courthouse. A couple of others who stayed back in the yard, proceeded to chat with her, eager to know more about this 'madman'.

While I was waiting for my turn at the witness box, I got a chance to see Sobhraj a little more closely. His dark eyes remained fixed; they stared straight at the judge, as if trying to gauge him.

Since I was sitting quite close on his left, I bent over, and said to him, 'Charles, I am Inspector Zende from Mumbai. I arrested you in 1971. Why do you do this? Why are you leading this kind of life?'

Sobhraj languidly turned his head to face me. Our eyes locked for an instant. His gaze, which appeared to be laser sharp only a moment ago, now looked at me very disdainfully.

'Please mind your own business,' he said with the same disdain, and returned to study the officiating judge.

In the witness box, I answered some routine questions about Sobhraj, my search for him, and the arrest in 1971.

My assigned work done, I came out of the courthouse, and walked towards my waiting wife. On the way, I was accosted and surrounded by some of the same people who had pronounced me a madman. They had heard my testimony and were now convinced that I was not delusional. They wanted to know more, to feel for themselves if my biceps were made of steel. They were a bit disappointed on that front. But Vijaya was suitably impressed by her husband. That is really all that mattered to me. We proceeded to enjoy a couple of days' sightseeing in the bracing Delhi autumn.

*

Sobhraj had been in Tihar Jail in the ten years since. All these memories passed through my mind as I learned of Sobhraj's escape from Tihar on 16 March 1986. I believed he would try to flee the country and would probably go back to places he had been to before—not that anyone was asking me.

Three days after his escape, while news about him was moving off the front pages, a reputed Mumbai tabloid, *Afternoon Despatch & Courier*, ran an article headlined, 'Zende: Mumbai Cop who arrested Sobhraj in 1971'. There were pictures of Sobhraj, me, and some of his doctored passports we had confiscated. The article was on the front page under a banner headline. Getting my picture in the newspaper was still a rare honour, and I bought a few extra copies for my collection and to share with friends.

On 2 April 1986, at about 9 a.m., I received a call from the Police Control Room. 'DGP Suryakant Jog saheb has called you urgently. Please meet him and Commissioner D.S. Soman saheb at 10 a.m. today at the Maharashtra Police Headquarters.'

There were 9,000 police inspectors in Maharashtra; they all reported to the director general of police (DGP) through a very, very long chain of command. Most inspectors never even got to see the DGP in their entire career, and I was being called to meet him urgently. What on earth had I done?

The DGP's office is on the first floor of the beautiful black and beige stone building at the start of Colaba Causeway. As was my habit, I reached about thirty minutes early, and visited my guru, DCP Arvind Patwardhan, whose office was on the ground floor of the same building. A deeply studious man, Patwardhan's office was always filled with police records and books.

'Come, Zende, I was expecting you,' he welcomed me in his usual matter-of-fact tone.

I told him why I was in the building.

'I am not surprised. You certainly know Sobhraj better than anyone else in all of India today. So, it is natural that they would call you after that tip-off,' Patwardhan continued in his flat tone.

'Tip-off? What tip-off' I wondered aloud.

'It's not my place to discuss this. But I have no doubt you are going to arrest Sobhraj again soon. Don't keep them waiting. It's almost time for your meeting,' he said, and turned back to the file he was studying.

I put my uniform cap back on, and purposefully ascended the seventeen curving steps, two at a time, to the first floor. The high-ceilinged lobby to the DGP's office was filled with over 100 years' worth of memorabilia, and pictures of some of the greatest police officers in our history.

Commissioner Soman and Joint Commissioner R.H. Mendonca were in the room. I struck my smartest salute. They ushered me into the DGP's conference room. The enormous, heavy mahogany table was flanked by uniformed officers. Some of them were from the Railway Police. Most of them wore 'collars', the black clip on their uniform's collar that identified them as officers of deputy commissioner rank and above—at least two levels above me. A few of my peer-level officers were standing at the back.

DGP Suryakant Jog sat at the head of the table. A trim, avuncular-faced man, his twinkling eyes and thick moustache were known to veil a sharp mind and a no-nonsense bias for action. The chair at the opposite end of the table was empty.

'Come, come, Zende. We are all eagerly waiting for you. Have a seat,' the DGP gestured towards an empty chair.

As soon as I had settled in, he continued.

'I read the story of you arresting Charles Sobhraj in the *Afternoon*, Zende. Very interesting. Can you please tell us the story in your own words? Take your time.'

It took me about fifteen minutes. My normal talking voice is quite loud, and I tend to use my face and hands quite liberally while talking. There were a few smiles as everyone listened carefully to what I had to say.

Once I was done, DGP Jog turned to the DCP of the Railway Police, Ambalal Verma, a slightly chubby man with thin-rimmed glasses.

'Verma saab, can you please tell Zende what your team has learnt?'

'Certainly, Jog saab. Thank you,' said Mr Verma, as he took over.

'On 29 March, Head Constable Kshirsagar saw a suspicious looking man at VT (Victoria Terminus) station. He was about to board the Gorakhpur Express. Constables Waghmare, Sasane and Kshirsagar checked the man's belongings. They found a locally made revolver, fifteen live cartridges and a military style hand-grenade. They interrogated the man for a long time, but he refused to say a word. They dug deeper into his belongings, and found a crumpled receipt from Hotel Panchratna in Panvel from a few days ago. A team of the Railway Police led by Inspector Sankath went to Hotel Panchratna with this man. Panchratna is a small, but decent hotel, run by the owner, Sanjay Potdar. He turned out to be a resourceful man with a sharp mind. He immediately recognized this man.

'Mr Potdar told us that this man had indeed stayed at his hotel a few days ago. But he was not alone. There were a few other people with him, including two men who looked and acted like foreigners. But they had all left. They had one car and one motorcycle. The hotel's security guard noted the numbers of these vehicles in their book by the entrance. Our team checked the books and obtained those numbers. And since there was not much else to do, they asked Mr Potdar to call them or the local police in case any of those people showed up again.

'The very next day, one of them, Devdutt Tyagi, came back to the hotel, and asked for his friends. Mr Potdar very shrewdly informed the man that his friends had gone out for some time. He allotted the man a room and offered him lunch. While he was eating, Mr Potdar called the local police. They came in, and promptly took Tyagi into custody. They interrogated him about who he was and what he was doing there, but Tyagi was a clamshell, refusing to open up. So they brought him to our office at VT.

'At VT, my team and I interrogated him. After a lot of persistent inquiry, he finally broke down, and blurted, "Why are you doing this to me? I am not part of Charles Sobhraj's plans, nor did I escape from Tihar with him. I only helped him escape."

'The name Sobhraj was like a bombshell of course, and we doubled our efforts to learn more from him,' Verma said.

The story went that after escaping from Tihar, Tyagi drove Sobhraj to Surat in Gujarat. Then he and their group went to five other places to meet accomplices and make further plans—Alwar in Rajasthan; Ahmedabad and Baroda in Gujarat; Goa; and Mumbai. While in Mumbai, Sobhraj said that for their future plans, it would be better if they moved around as part of a couple, rather than in a large group of men. He had a lawyer in Delhi, Sneh Sengar. He had one earring of hers. Sobhraj gave Tyagi that earring to facilitate introductions, asked him to go to Delhi, and to bring Sneh Sengar and a couple of her female friends with him. But Sengar refused, and Tyagi had to come back alone.

'When we heard this story, and Sobhraj's association with this man, we immediately called DGP Jog,' said Verma.

Jog thanked him and turned to me again.

'Zende, what do you think? You probably know Sobhraj better than any of us.'

'Sir, in my view, Sobhraj probably knows that Tyagi has been arrested, and has told us all this. Ordinarily, a criminal would not go back to the places he has already been to if he knows that the police are aware where he has been. But Sobhraj is not like that. He has a very poor opinion of Indian police. If he had reason to go to these places, he will likely go back there. So, I think we should send teams to each of these places. Especially Goa. It is quite likely that Sobhraj will try to leave the country, and Goa is the best place for that. Since it has so many international hippie travellers, it is also a place where Sobhraj may try to commit a crime or two before leaving.'

'Okay, I agree. Who do you want on your team?' the DGP dove into action.

'My team, sir? For what, sir?' I asked, flummoxed.

'Look, let's not waste time. What you are saying makes sense to me. Let's send teams to each of these places. I want you to lead the team to Goa. Leave today. Take a few officers.'

'Thank you, sir. That would be an honour. But sir, there is one more thing. Sobhraj always stays in the best hotels. To maximize our chances of finding him, our teams should also stay in the Taj or other top hotels in these places.'

'I agree, Zende,' DGP Jog said and then turned to the joint commissioner of the Crime Branch, R.H. Mendonca.

'Mr Mendonca, will you please manage this? Money should not be a constraint for this. The Goa team should leave today. Please book flight tickets for Zende. The rest of the team can drive down.'

The DGP turned to me again, and said, 'Good luck, Zende. Keep me posted.' He flashed a warm, wide grin, with a twinkle in his eyes, and left the room.

Once he had left, Commissioner Soman spoke up. 'Let us all head back to my office, and we can take it forward from there. Zende, do you have a vehicle?'

'I have my scooter, sir.'

'Very good, let's leave.' Turning to Verma, he added, 'Mr Verma, we will be in touch soon. This would not have been possible without your help.'

On my way back, my mind was abuzz with thoughts. It would have been so good to have some of my former colleagues like Inspector Prabhakar Sawant and Inspector 'Dinya' Akolkar, who were involved in the 1971 arrest with me. But Sawant had retired. Maybe Akolkar could lead another team. I would recommend that. Who else could we add to the team? How should I approach this task?

It was so amazing that the DGP had thought of me in this situation. And he had not sat in his office and delegated the responsibility— he had swung into action, called me in directly and spoken to a junior officer like me so respectfully. These were great leadership traits. Would I really be flying to Goa? I had never sat in a plane before. Okay I did once, fifteen years ago, for twenty minutes. And would I actually stay in a five-star hotel in Goa? That would be another first.

Before I knew it, I was at the commissioner's office compound on L.T. Marg. This complex of buildings also housed the Crime Branch office where I had worked before, and I was in familiar surroundings.

I went to Mr Mendonca's office. He first placed a call to Commissioner Soman.

'Zende, I hope you are ready to leave,' Commissioner Soman said. 'The flight is at 4 p.m. today. The tickets are being booked. I have spoken to Ajit Kerkar, CEO of Taj Hotels. There is a cottage booked for you at the Taj Hermitage. It is their top property in Goa. Please take this pouch. It has 10,000 rupees. Please use the money carefully. You can plan to be there for about a week. We will decide plans after that. I will let you discuss further details with Mr Mendonca. Keep me posted at all times.'

'Thank you very much, sir,' I replied. 'I have one request. There is no telling what network of accomplices Sobhraj may have in Goa. He may recognize or remember my name. I think I should use an alias, including for my hotel bookings. The whole team should travel in plainclothes only, to blend in with the crowd.'

'That makes sense.'

'I will go under the name of Shashi Raut; it's a common name and will not stand out.'

The name I had chosen was that of a car thief I had arrested years ago; it had been the first that popped into my mind as I thought of an alias.

'Shashi Raut. That works. It's easy to remember. Good luck, Zende. Hope you are successful,' said the commissioner, and rang off.

I stayed with Mr Mendonca, who was the officer in-charge of the Crime Branch. He asked me, 'Zende, who else do you want on your team? I think we will need to include Railway Inspector Sankath, who did the excellent initial work.'

'I would like to take Sub-Inspector Bagwan, sir. We have done a lot of work together, and he is also good with weapons, if things get messy.'

'No, not Bagwan. Take Amolik. He is with the Crime Branch and is a better fit.'

'As you say, sir.'

We talked for a bit longer, and then I took my leave. Just as I was about to leave, Mr Mendonca dropped a bombshell.

'You know, Zende, I have been thinking ... You are very good at interrogating people and making connections. You should stay here in Mumbai. Let Senior Railway Inspector Shrotri lead the Goa team.'

I was terribly disappointed, but I had to obey my senior officer's orders.

'Whatever you say, sir,' I said, and left his office.

All the plans I had been making on my scooter ride to his office now lay shattered, including the possibility of flying on a plane.

But DGP Jog had asked me to go, and he certainly needed to be informed about this change in plans. I turned around and went back to Mr Mendonca's room.

'Sir, will you please inform Jog saheb about the change in plans?'

Mr Mendonca was pensive for a moment. Then he said, 'No. Let's stick to the original plan. You go to Goa.'

I did a mental cartwheel, and before there was any further discussion, saluted my senior officer, and went straight home to pack for the trip of my life.

It was about noon when I got home. I had to pack and leave in an hour. Our children were at home with Vijaya; it was the summer holidays at school. My family had almost never seen me come back home so early from work, and were quite surprised to see me this excited. While Vijaya packed my bags, I grabbed a bite and shared my plans. They would probably not hear from me for the next few days, and needed to know what was going on. I had no fear that they would let anything slip to anyone. Keeping such secrets is second nature to families of policemen. There was a lot of excitement about so many things. Top of the list was of course the possibility of rearresting Sobhraj, whose incredible jailbreak was scarcely two weeks old. But the flight, the trip to Goa where the fish would be amazing, doing a covert operation where I would have an alias, and the possibility of eating Alphonso mangoes early were all excitedly discussed by my family.

The flight was on time. A car and driver from the Taj Hermitage were waiting to pick up Shashi Raut. The name was going to take some getting used to, and this was useful practice. Since everything had been arranged from the top, I was treated like a VIP, and taken directly to my cottage. It was beyond doubt the best hotel room I had ever stayed in, with its own private pool. It was still only about 8 p.m., so I took a walk near the hotel to get a sense of Goa. I could not waste time, and I used the walk to plan our manhunt.

The likeliest places that Sobhraj would show up were those frequented by foreign tourists. They were convenient places for meeting any international accomplices, and to find travellers, who were his preferred victims.

The hotel bar was a good place for this, especially if he was staying there. I put on some beach-style clothes and a pair of sunglasses, so as to be less recognizable.

Luckily, wearing sunglasses even in the dimly lit bar was not uncommon here. I kept up this practice of being at the bar whenever there was no better place to watch for Sobhraj.

The next morning, Amolik and Sankath reported to me, and we decided to fan out across Goa. We could not share Sobhraj's name to avoid raising suspicions. From the records of Hotel Panchratna, we knew that Sobhraj and Hall were riding on a motorcycle, with the number plate GOR 5490. It was possible they were still using it.

Goa's local transport system was quite unorganized, and unique. Many tourists who travelled alone loved to hitch rides on motorcycle taxis. Their riders, called pilots, were very competitive, and drove rashly, much like motorcycle racers. They also took pride in their bikes, and new bikes—usually customized in some way—were shown off with much pride. These pilots, who waited for pillion riders at specific spots across Goa, were more likely to have noticed other motorcycles. It was with them that we began our inquiry about Sobhraj's motorcycle. Our story was that my brother had stolen the bike and run away from home. We were naturally keener on finding the brother than the bike.

We were driving around Goa's popular tourist spots in the car Amolik and Sankath had driven in from Mumbai. In each major town, we would park the car, and fan out to scout possible hiding spots, and inquire with the 'pilots' about the 'missing' bike.

Another possible lead we had to check was international calls. In those days, there was no ISD calling—you could not just dial with a '+' or '00' followed by a country code to call overseas. You had to call the local telephone exchange and request them to connect you. The number of telephone connections available to make such calls were limited, and there was a lot of waiting if you wanted to place an overseas call. Hotels typically charged a very high premium for these international calls. So, people who wanted to make an overseas call would go to a bar with a phone, place a request, and wait over a few drinks for the call to connect. It was good business for the bars. And they were in no rush to get the calls connected. While there were several bars in Goa that offered this facility, all calls were routed through one place, the Goa Telephone Exchange. If we got a list of all the calls that had been placed over the last few days, we could use those threads to find Sobhraj.

On 3 April, we went to the Telephone Exchange in the capital, Panaji. I approached the general manager and informed him of our true intent. He was very helpful, and requested his deputy, Mr Menezies to help us. He heard us out patiently, and then politely spoke.

'Forgive me, sir, but you are in the wrong place.'

'What do you mean, Mr Menezies?' I asked, confused.

'You see. Given your description of Sobhraj as a wily and well-informed man, if money is not a constraint, he will not bother with the telephone exchange. He will place a lightning call.'

'What on earth is a lightning call?' I wondered.

'If you can get a priority line at your establishment, then you can call international almost immediately.'

'Wow! There is such a facility? Do all bars have it?'

'Unfortunately, it's quite difficult and expensive to get this connection. Only one bar in Goa has it—O'Coqueiro in Porvorim, which is not far from here on the Mapusa highway. They take care of some of our exchange employees, who maintain this facility for them. My advice would be to wait for Sobhraj in that bar. He is likely to come there if he is in Goa,' said Menezies.

This was an incredible piece of information. We decided to stake out O'Coqueiro every day.

We were also visiting the various beaches in turn. Since we wanted to maintain a low profile, we did not get too many people on the job and tried our best to keep our expenses low, so that the 10,000 rupees I had been given could last as long as possible.

We also kept up our canvassing among the motorcycle pilots. We had asked dozens of them, with no success, but we kept at it.

On 4 April, we visited Mapusa, the biggest town in north Goa, with a good mix of communities and a bustling market place. It was also famous for the Milagres Church and the Bodgeshwar Temple. As we were driving around, we passed a beautiful looking Hanuman Temple. In the square outside the temple, there were a few motorcycle pilots sheltering in the shadow of a banyan tree. We made our usual enquiries with the oldest-looking of the young men.

The youth I was speaking to shook his head disinterestedly. We were used to this response, and after a couple of follow-up questions, started to walk away. A whiny, much younger voice stopped us in our tracks.

'*Kite khota bolton re* (You are such a liar)!' said a spindly boy, probably no more than seventeen. I was sure he was not even allowed to legally ride a motorized vehicle. Perhaps he repaired bikes.

'What do you mean? Why would I lie?' I responded.

'See! The bike is very easy to spot. It is a bright peacock blue colour. It's a brand-new bike and does not even have a chain cover. From the expression on your face, I can tell that you don't even know this basic information about the bike.'

The others in the group sniggered at this last remark.

'You mean you have seen it? Of course, I know!'

'The riders are foreigners. One is white and the other looks like a Nepali. Neither can be your brother. And most important, the series GOR has never been launched in Goa. So, the number plates are clearly fake,' said the youth.

I was dumbstruck. This boy's observation skills and knowledge of his trade were incredible. And he had provided us with a clear clue that Sobhraj was indeed in Goa. The Westerner with him was probably David Hall.

I controlled my urge to hug the boy, but instead let my shoulders droop, feigning disappointment.

We were tightening the noose around Sobhraj and needed more people on the team to get our man before he escaped. I headed to a place from where I could call Mumbai, and dialled Joint Commissioner Mendonca.

'Sir, I think we are in the right place. Sobhraj is certainly in Goa. I need more men.'

'That's great news, Zende. Tell me what happened,' said Mr Mendonca, echoing my excitement.

I told him about the conversation with the pilot boy.

'That's fantastic. How many men do you need? And do you have any recommendations?'

Naturally, I wanted to get a couple of people that I had worked with before, and could rely on.

'Sir, Sub-Inspector Satam, who worked with me in Dharavi, and Sub-Inspector Salunkhe, who worked with me in the Crime Branch would be great.'

'Done. I will also send two more sub-inspectors, and Inspector Shashi Kamat with them.'

'That is very kind, sir. When can they reach here? We cannot waste time.'

'They should be with you tomorrow morning for sure.'

'Okay, sir. Sooner the better. Thank you, sir,' I said and hung up.

After the call, we went to our stake-out at O'Coqueiro. It was a large property just off the main highway. The restaurant itself was like an old Goan house, painted white. It was located in a large compound filled with trees. This provided ample parking for the cars and was a draw on the busy thoroughfare. Before entering the restaurant, you passed through a long veranda, with a white railing, and old-fashioned black- and cream-coloured tiles. You could sit at two-seater tables in the veranda, and observe the people coming and going, or you could enjoy the music, hustle-bustle, and food and drinks in the main restaurant. Their authentic Goan food, especially the chicken cafreal, were immensely popular.

'Shashi Raut' and his team spent a good portion of 5 April in O'Coqueiro. There was a strong reason to think that Sobhraj would come here. Naturally, he had no reason to wait in Goa, so it would probably not be a long wait for us. But every minute seemed like ages. All we could do was wait. We had to order enough food and drinks, so as to not raise suspicion. Also, we could not drink much alcohol or eat heavy food, as it would make us drowsy. It helped that I had quit alcohol ten years ago.

We waited and watched. The only piece of good news we got that day was that the team had left from Mumbai in two cars and would reach late that night or early next morning. I had asked for them to meet me as soon as they had reached.

That night, I slept fitfully. Finally, in the wee hours, I stepped onto my cottage's balcony. It was a beautiful space, with a lovely front garden, and a private pool that I had barely even noticed. It was a lovely summer night, and in the early morning light, I could see Venus shining bright. I love watching the sky and observing the various constellations in motion. It is wonderful to see what a vast universe we are all a part of. It calmed me down and, reassured about myself, I went back to bed.

In those early morning hours, I had the most vivid and beautiful dream. I was riding a motorbike. After riding for a while, the bike took off like a helicopter, and we flew through the air till I noticed a cheering crowd below me. The bike then flew down, and gently landed in a chowk. It was one I had seen before—the one outside the Mapusa Hanuman Temple. The crowd had been cheering for me. Once I landed, they ran up to me and garlanded me several times. I woke up feeling euphoric—my grandmother used to say that early morning dreams foretell the future.

It was Sunday, and there would even be lunch crowds at O'Coqueiro. I planned to be at the restaurant all day today. Sobhraj was known to operate in south-east Asia too, so he might make calls even during the day, or later in the day if he was trying to connect with accomplices in the West. We had to watch O'Coqueiro at all times.

After a late breakfast, I noticed my former colleagues, Satam and Salunkhe approaching. They instinctively started to salute me, but caught themselves, and adjusted their hair instead. It was a funny sight, and we all exchanged smiles. They were accompanied by an older man, who would be Inspector Shashi Kamat.

I asked them about their journey and told them we would start at 10 a.m. at O'Coqueiro.

'Saheb, it was a rough long journey. Can we catch up on some sleep first?' said one of them.

'Look, I understand. But this is an important day,' I replied. 'Let's not forget how much the state is spending on our being here. Let's make sure we don't waste this opportunity.'

'I understand, Zende,' replied Kamat, the senior-most member of the group.

We reached O'Coqueiro and took up positions to avoid being too prominent. It also helped us cover different sections of the sprawling bungalow-like restaurant. That evening, there was an India–Pakistan hockey match being telecast live on TV. In those pre-IPL and T20 days, hockey had more support than it does now. Goa had a hockey culture, having contributed some Olympians. A good crowd was expected. That would make it easier for us to blend in, but on the other hand, a crowd would be tricky to handle and protect in case things got out of hand. To complicate matters further, we noticed some signage indicating there was a wedding party also planned for that evening. Preparations for that were in full swing.

The wedding party would occupy the middle section of the restaurant, with only a couple of other tables available for public use. That's where the TV was. Our officers took up positions at a table close to the TV and the entrance. They would be less prominent, posing as hockey enthusiasts. They ordered a drink or two and kept watering it down with water or soda. I spent most of my time in a spot from where I could keep an eye on the people getting out of the cars and entering the compound. My position also made it easy for me to quickly catch the eye of my officers. Then, we waited.

Waiting is a tough game, especially if you are waiting for someone you are eager to meet but are not sure will turn up. The arrival of every person was like a shot of dopamine. I would look without seeming too interested. I had last seen Sobhraj about ten years ago. He was known to wear caps and sunglasses to disguise himself. April in Goa is extremely hot. So, almost everyone walking into this expensive tourist hotspot was wearing either a cap or sunglasses. These repeated doses of dopamine, with the accompanying stress, made the wait exhausting. But being tired was not an option. At times like this, I play little games to keep myself alert. So, as I sat sipping my soft drink, I counted the number of cars of each brand or type as they entered, noting which state the tourist vehicles were from, etc. The tourist buses were of less interest to me. Hindustan Motors Ambassadors and Premier Padminis dominated the count. Most of these cars would enter the compound, where passengers would alight near the entrance to the restaurant, after which the driver would proceed to park the car and wait. There was ample parking.

By about 8 p.m., the hockey match and the wedding party were both in full swing. India had taken the lead, so spirits were high. Even our officers were quite engaged in the game. On the other hand, like so many Goan wedding parties, the one at O'Coqueiro was a spirited one with much singing and dancing. It kept the place lively and helped us fight fatigue.

At about 10.30 p.m., another Fiat showed up and two men alighted. One was a Caucasian-looking Westerner, wearing rumpled shorts and a round-necked T-shirt. He had a moustache and looked like an affluent beach bum. The other man was not tall, but had an impressive lithe physique, and walked quickly. He wore a golf-cap pulled a little low over his eyes, full-length black trousers, and a light-coloured shirt. He was carrying a small briefcase. I recognized him instantly.

The ten years of not having seen Sobhraj fell away in an instant. Our quarry was here. My heart raced. I feigned disinterest and looked over at their car. The parking was relatively full, and I noted that the driver had to go some distance. He was a swarthy, middle-aged man, with blank eyes.

Sobhraj and his accomplice, probably David Hall, settled down at a table in the veranda and ordered a round of drinks. Sobhraj's gaze kept darting about. I could not risk him spotting and recognizing me. Besides, I needed a plan to nab him.

I got up and casually sauntered over to a table directly behind him, standing in the shadow of a pillar from where I could watch his movements while still remaining concealed. On my way to him, I took a pen and paper from a waiter and noted down my plan, and instructions to each officer. I called a waiter over, told him briefly who I was, and asked him to hand over the paper to my team.

Sobhraj could not see the team from where he was seated, and did not see them disperse. Satam and Sankath walked over to his car to make sure the driver did not intercede. Salunkhe went out to keep a watch. Kamat and Amolik came over to my table, not far from where Sobhraj sat, and stayed alert.

Satam and Sankath had their backs towards me, so I could not see what passed between them and Sobhraj's driver. But clearly, it had not gone well, because the driver got out of the car and started walking towards the restaurant.

If the driver got to Sobhraj and alerted him, there would be hell to pay. We could not preclude the possibility of Sobhraj and Hall pulling out a weapon, or even taking a hostage or two from the wedding party. In turn, the driver's action dispelled any remaining doubt about Sobhraj's identity. And then suddenly, my dream from that morning came back to me. It had certainly foretold something good for me, and this was my moment.

I sprang from my chair and strode towards their table; as mentioned before, Sobhraj's back was to me, and Hall was not looking either. Amolik and Kamat trailed behind me at a short distance.

Without any second thought, I got to Sobhraj, put my arms around him tightly.

'Hello, Charles, how are you?' I asked in my best mocking voice.

I could feel Sobhraj straining hard against my grip, squirming to get loose. He was a martial arts expert, but the element of surprise meant I had the upper hand.

'What nonsense!' he managed to yell back. 'Who is Charles?'

'Don't pretend. I am the same Zende who caught you in 1971. I know you are bloody Charles Sobhraj!'

My loud voice carried the name of Charles Sobhraj well over the sounds of the TV and the wedding party, and everyone stopped what they were doing to witness the drama unfold.

Amolik and Kamat were now standing next to me. I noticed Hall reaching for a knife strapped to his thigh and Sobhraj lunged towards his briefcase.

'Amolik ... bag!' I shouted. He quickly grabbed the bag before Sobhraj could, while Kamat wrested the knife from Hall.

Amolik opened the bag and found a loaded pistol in it.

'Saheb, this is a loaded gun. He could have killed people if he had got the bag. Let's finish the bastard right here,' said Amolik, clearly alarmed and angry.

'No, we will do no such thing. We will take him back to Mumbai.'

By now the others—Satam, Sankath and Salunkhe—had joined us. Between us, we got a tighter grip on our prisoners.

The ruckus that had been caused had caught the attention of many people, and several of the wedding guests surrounded us as did the manager of the restaurant, Mr Viegas, who broke through their cordon and came forward.

'Kamat, please work with the manager and get whatever twine and ropes they have. As much as possible,' I said.

In five minutes, we had several bundles of jute twine and plastic rope at our disposal. We set to work. We first pulled Sobhraj's arms behind his back and tied them in place. Then we tied his legs at the ankles. We did the same to Hall and immobilized them both. Then we laid them down and tied them from head to toe. We could afford to take no risks with this duo, especially Sobhraj. The man was a wily, ruthless killer and an escape artist.

Once he was tied up, we dispersed the crowd to create a passage. Three of us picked up Sobhraj, and three took Hall. Neither was very heavy, and they seemed to know they had no means of escape. We shoved one each in two cars—on the floor of the back seat—and two people sat on the back seat of each car, with their feet firmly planted on them.

I rushed back to the restaurant and placed a lightning call to Commissioner Soman.

'Sir, the work is done!'

'WHAT! You mean you caught Charles Sobhraj? Are you sure?'

'Not hundred per cent sure, sir, one thousand per cent sure!'

'This is amazing, Zende. Congratulations! I am so proud of you!'

'Thank you very much, sir. What shall we do now? There are only a few of us, and we have small cars. Shall we take the help of Goa Police?'

'No! No! Leave right now. Don't stop anywhere. Get him here right away. I will come down and receive you at my office.'

While I was on the phone, Kamat and the others had phoned the rest of the team who were still at the hotel. They rushed to O'Coqueiro. I got into the car with Sobhraj. Now, there were three people in the back seat of each car. We grabbed a small meal at Mapusa and set off on a non-stop drive to Mumbai.

What an evening! In an hour, we had gone from an endless wait for a dreaded serial-killer on the loose to having him trussed up in our car. I was dripping with sweat. My throat was hoarse from shouting and the excitement; endorphins and adrenaline were racing through my veins.

We sped towards Mumbai in the dark of the night. It was a twelve-hour journey but we made only two stops to fuel up, and to relieve ourselves. The captured duo had to relieve themselves into bottles.

None of us had slept well in days, and we knew we still had a long way to go, so we splashed water on our faces and sang songs to keep ourselves awake and alert. I have a terrible singing voice, but I know songs from my time in the Rashtra Seva Dal, and even marching songs from my time in the police school. We sang *'Jai*

jai Maharashtra mazha' and '*Mazhi ladki Susheela*', apart from many old Hindi songs.

In the early hours of dawn, as we drove through Poladpur, we witnessed a beautiful sight up ahead on the Sahyadri Hills—the legendary Raigad Fort of Chhatrapati Shivaji Maharaj. This was the place he had been crowned king, after beating back the Mughals and the Adilshahis from Maharashtra. This struggle for freedom had preceded India's own freedom struggle by a few hundred years. My heart was filled with pride for my motherland. I too had won a small battle by capturing this enemy of our country. Unwittingly, I spouted, 'Maharaj, today this simple Mavla soldier has captured a great enemy of the people. Please bless me!' My voice shook with emotion and filled me with renewed energy as we followed the rising sun towards Mumbai.

At about 11 a.m., we entered Panvel. Several police vehicles were waiting for us. They had come to relieve us. We handed over Sobhraj and Hall to them. Our team was instructed to drive straight to the DGP's office in Colaba. We took a few moments to see our prisoners being secured in the police van. Then, the entire team heaved a big, collective sigh of relief. We didn't have time to rest, though. A lot of very senior police officers were waiting for us so, we zoomed towards south Mumbai.

We reached the DGP's office to a bigger welcome than we could have imagined. Commissioner Soman had come downstairs to greet and congratulate us. We were all sweaty and grimy, dressed in the same plain clothes that we had been wearing for nearly twenty-four hours now. We were welcomed with a hearty smile by DGP Jog himself. Ordinarily, none of us would have dreamed of appearing before him in anything but our full uniform. There were throngs of journalists from every major publication, and he humbly took the proverbial back seat as my team and I described our Goa adventure. As the leader of the team, I became the face of the Charles Sobhraj arrest story. Since I had arrested him a second time, it became quite a sensation.

'Zendebad', screamed the newspaper *Daily* the next morning. That has got to be my favourite newspaper headline of all time. On 8 April, almost every newspaper featured the same story on its front page. In bold, supersized font, the sort that would be reserved for a Cricket World Cup win or an Olympic Gold, they all proclaimed the sensational arrest of the serial-killing human monster, Charles Sobhraj.

The early news articles that appeared in the afternoon tabloids on 7 April featured a hilarious and very imaginative version of events, where the team was described as having dressed up as waiters in O'Coqueiro to arrest Sobhraj. After interviewing us at the Maharashtra Police Headquarters, most media then carried the correct version of events. The evening news on national television featured me describing the events in my Marathi-laced Hindi—something my family still teases me about.

The newspaper headlines and TV interviews were only the start. Almost every news magazine featured the story on its cover, with a photograph of yours truly in a crumpled, grimy maroon shirt, which I have retained as a memento.

For months after that, there were endless interviews and speeches. There were so many visitors, journalists and bouquets in our house that my family literally had to move to the neighbours' house to take a moment's respite from making chai for the guests.

When I went back to work at my post in Agripada police station, there was an impromptu celebration at the compound. I was literally carried on people's shoulders like a star sportsman.

The Prime Minister of India and his ministers invited me to meet them, as did the chief minister of Maharashtra. The state governor conferred a special award in person. India's greatest singers, the sisters Lata Mangeshkar and Asha Bhosle, organized a special felicitation on the occasion of their father Dinanath Mangeshkar's birthday, just to hear my story. Lata didi talked about how happy she felt when, for the first (and only) time, the Amul hoarding outside her home was in Marathi—'Atakepaar Zende!' This was a pun on the peak of the Maratha empire, where Raghodada was able to win territories as far away as Atak in Afghanistan. Interestingly, that hoarding riffed off the version of events where we had dressed as waiters.

Pune's venerated Dagdusheth Halwai Ganpati Trust crafted a rare panchdhatu (alloy of five metals) idol of Ganpati as a gift for me, and it was handed over to me by the legendary shehnai player Ustad Bismillah Khan. The event was attended by thousands who listened to my story with rapt attention.

The crowning glory perhaps came at Doke Talim in Nana Peth, Pune, where I grew up. Thousands of people welcomed and felicitated me. The love and adulation were overwhelming, and I feel eternally grateful for it.

This love and respect from the public felt akin to the glory of a goal-scorer who gets almost all the appreciation. But behind that glorious moment, there is always a large team and years of practice and preparation.

5

SHAKTI'S PRODUCER IS KIDNAPPED!

It was the day of Lakshmi Puja. Diwali celebrations were in full swing in most parts of Mumbai. The Mumbai Police had to organize extra bandobust to main the peace. The exuberant celebrations were occasionally marred by skirmishes between revellers—disputes over over-enthusiastic celebrations, or fireworks that were set-off dangerously—that acquired an edge when fuelled by alcohol. After Ganpati, this is the most widely celebrated festival in Mumbai. Of course, for us cops, that means late nights at work.

I was posted at Crime Branch as a senior inspector. Around 10 p.m., having made sure most of the hotspots were stable, I told the duty officer that I was heading home. He knew he could call me if anything untoward happened.

Every year, my wife, Vijaya, prepares the most scrumptious sweet and savoury faraal—chakli, besan laddoos, shankarpali, and her magnum opus, the Marathi favourite, karanji. Making karanjis is a painstaking affair. Three layers of dough, delicately filled with a delicious dry coconut stuffing and carefully fried to a golden colour. Every crunchy bite is like a burst of flavour in the mouth. I was looking forward to the evening with my family and enjoying some of Vijaya's homemade delicacies after we had done the puja.

When I walked into the house, my fourteen-year-old son was sitting with a plateful of faraal in front of him, oblivious to his mother's chidings. 'Nishu, this is your third karanji. What will I feed the guests? Kantibhai will come tomorrow. He will want his box of karanjis as usual,' she told him.

Several of our friends and people whom I might have helped as part of my job would visit us with Diwali mithai and dry-fruit boxes. Some of the regulars would not only eat Vijaya's special karanji, but also pack some for their families. Many of our visitors brought dry-fruit boxes as gifts for us. They were a standard feature of Diwali gifting. Packed like bento boxes, with about twelve pockets, each pocket containing 50–100 grams of dry fruits or nuts. However, on that day, I noticed my son also had a really large dry-fruit box with him. As soon as he saw me, he excitedly asked, 'Pappa, who are Mushir and Riaz? Just look at the box they have sent. Each packet is like half a kilo of dry fruit. I have tried them all. The salted cashew is top quality,' said Nishu, a self-declared cashew connoisseur.

'Arre, you have forgotten?' I teased him. 'Do you remember that private movie screening of the film *Shakti* we went to? Mushir and Riaz produced that movie.'

'How can I forget *Shakti*, Pappa? The movie was shot in my school. And it has the biggest pairing in Hindi cinema ever—Amitabh Bachchan and Dilip Kumar together in one movie. Sorry, but that totally beats Dilip Kumar and Prithviraj Kapoor in *Mughal-e-Azam*. That scene where they meet, and the sea is raging in the background ... that's never going to grow old.'

I laughed and told him that the backdrop against which the movie was released was way more tumultuous than that sea. Mushir, especially, was lucky to be alive to see the release of his movie. Our team did some amazing work there. And some of the follow-up action changed the face of Mumbai crime forever.

I told him that Mushir Alam and Mohammed Riaz were brothers-in-law; Mushir was married to Riaz's sister. They were business partners too. Their family owned Model Tanneries which was a very respected business in Kanpur. The city had been a big leather production and export centre since the days of the East India Company. The modern-day Uttar Pradesh state had a large military presence during the British Raj, and they needed leather supplies like saddles, belts and stirrups. The multi-tiered caste population in the area meant there was an ecosystem suitable for skinning the animals, tanning the hide, manufacturing them into useful products, and selling them to the army, and later to the world. Model

Tanneries was one of the biggest names with one of the tallest chimneys.

Mushir and Riaz carried that success to the Mumbai film industry with their Mushir-Riaz Productions. The duo's soft-spoken manner and savvy business sense had yielded hit films like *Safar* and *Bairaag*.

In 1980, they had launched their biggest movie yet, with some of the biggest names in Indian cinema at the time. The script was written by Salim–Javed; R.D. Burman composed the music; it was edited by M.S. Shinde, and directed by Ramesh Sippy. This was the same iconic team that had made the superhit film, *Sholay*.

Shakti was obviously a big-budget production—the amount probably ran into the crores. Films and criminal gangs were notoriously intertwined those days. Criminals could get their money laundered through films, and since films are not considered an industry, such dirty money was sometimes a convenient way to finance a film. Given their own flourishing leather business in Kanpur, perhaps Mushir-Riaz Productions did not have to depend on the gangs to finance their movie. Whatever the reason, two up-and-coming criminals, Alamzeb and Amirzada, heard rumours that Mushir had brought in a large sum of money in cash to Mumbai. That was an astronomical sum, and they wanted a piece of it.

The film was ready. Promotions were in full flow. The media was abuzz since the magnum opus was slated to release in eight days. Mushir had been working long hours to make sure everything was in place for the biggest investment of his life to be a success. At around 11 p.m., about a week before the release of the film, he stepped out of his office, clad in his trademark white pants and full-sleeved white shirt. His slim frame slipped comfortably into the back seat of his Mercedes. It was good to be rich.

His driver, Waseem, a trusted man from Kanpur, was familiar with Mumbai roads. '*Bhai sahab, bahut badi* hit *hogi film. Koi shaq nahin hai* (Brother, the film will be a huge hit, there's no doubt),' the driver told the producer.

'*Inshallah* (God willing), Waseem!' Mushir replied.

The brightly lit lanes of Mumbai were an integral part of his film, and as they eased along, Mushir reminisced about the scenes shot on some of them. As they crossed Arthur Road, a Premier Padmini zoomed out of a side lane. Waseem swerved just in time to avoid hitting it, and in true Kanpur style, jumped out to deal with the three occupants of the 'crappy desi car'. This was just the moment Amirzada and Alamzeb were waiting for. As soon as Waseem stepped out, Amirzada ran up to Mushir's car, yanked open the door on his side, and pulled him out.

'*Ae, kaun hai tu* (Who are you)?' yelled Mushir.

Before he could say anything else, Amirzada clamped a hand over his mouth. '*Awaaj nahin mangta hai idhar, samjha na* (Don't you dare make a sound, got it)?'

Waseem turned towards the assailants. But one blow to his head left him out cold. Alamzeb and Amirzada, members of the Pathan gang, were acting in tandem now. They dragged Mushir's slim, struggling body into the Padmini, and zoomed off. They blindfolded and tied him up.

'*Bhai, kya chahiye aapko. Main koi gunda nahin hoon. Kya kar rahe ho aap*? (Brother, what do you want? I am not a gangster. What are you up to?)' Mushir asked. But the criminals did not reply. A knifepoint at his throat ensured he would not utter any more words of protest.

In what seemed like a few minutes of reckless driving through winding lanes, they reached their destination. Two pairs of strong, callused hands hauled Mushir out. He was carried up a flight of stairs, and then another. He heard a heavy metal bolt move, and then a door creaked open. He was unceremoniously thrown on to the floor like a sack of potatoes. Then, the kicking began, on his legs and back. Slaps across his face. Punches to his head and chest. Mushir was in a panic. Being from Kanpur, he had seen some rough guys, but never at such close quarters. In a short while, he realized that even though they were hitting him, it was not very hard.

The men who had carried him so easily would have no difficulty in breaking a few bones if they really meant to hurt him. No, these guys were only trying to scare him.

Mushir recovered his composure enough to blurt out, '*Bas karo*! Stop it! For the sake of Allah, stop! What do you want?'

They stopped and peeled off his blindfold. Two hulking men stood in front of him. A couple of others stood guard by the door of the small dark room.

'*Apun Amirzada. Naam toh suna hoga. Aur ye hai Alamzeb* (I am Amirzada, you must've heard the name. And this is Alamzeb).'

Mushir did not bother keeping tabs on the who's who of the underworld, but these names had become widely known for their brazen gun attack on Dawood Ibrahim. Mushir was now quaking in fear.

'Call Dilip Kumar!' Amirzada barked.

'Call Yusuf bhai?' asked Mushir, puzzled, and using Dilip Kumar's real name. 'At this time? Why?'

'Isn't that where you have stored your money? At his house?' Amirzada continued.

'What money, bhai? I don't know what you are talking about,' Mushir's voice was trembling, but in control.

One more slap made Mushir's ears ring.

'*Pachaas lakh!* I know you have fifty lakh in cash,' said the gangster.

Harish Sugandh, the proprietor of Glamour Studios, was the likely source of the rumour. Glamour was home to the photographers to the stars; several movies got their publicity shots done by them. The studio was really good at its job, and Harish knew how to massage egos to get plum assignments. He also knew the power of name-dropping, and chatting people up. It was crucial to the success of his business. The publicity shots of *Shakti* were also done by him. While bragging about this mega-budget film to somebody, he had possibly let slip that the producers were loaded businessmen from Kanpur and had brought in fifty lakh rupees for the last mile before the film's release. The word got around quickly. 'What's more, the money is in my garage,' Harish had boasted.

At this point, Alamzeb hurled an abuse at his partner, Amirzada. 'Ch*****, Amir. The money is not with Yusuf. It's with Harish. You never listen,' he scolded.

'Wherever they are! Mushir, enough is enough! Get us twenty-five lakh, right now!' thundered Amirzada.

'Look,' Mushir said, trying to steady his voice. He knew that at least there was no immediate danger to his life. It was a question of money. 'I don't have that kind of money. It has all been paid out. In fact, I have almost no money at all. It's all been spent on this enormous production. Leave me. If my movie is a hit, then I can give you some money.'

A few more slaps. Harder this time.

Amirzada doubted him. But now, he was beginning to doubt his own information too. 'You stay here for a couple of days. When you suffer without food and water, your brain will start working better. That will help you remember where your money is,' he told the producer.

They left Mushir there. Alone. The door was securely bolted from the outside, but his hands and legs remained tied. He sat alone on the floor of the musty room and noticed a packet of glucose biscuits lying not too far away. He could eat them if he could drag himself over and use his mouth creatively. But he was too tired, and drifted off to unconsciousness.

No one showed up the next morning. Not even when he screamed. Soon, he focused his attention on eating.

The biscuits gave him some strength, but not for long. He fell asleep again. When he woke up, he realized he had to relieve himself urgently. He yelled out. One of the goons who was guarding the door stormed in and shut him up. He pointed to a door across the very narrow hallway. Next to the door was an old calendar, which was probably still up on the wall only because it had a picture of Mecca's Kaaba on it. Mushir was allowed to do his business and immediately dragged back to his cell.

In the evening, he heard a faint sound—the voices of adolescent children. He recognized the tone and some of their words. They were chanting from the Quran. Was there a madrassa close by? He drifted into a stupor with the rhythmic drone of those chants.

A few hours later, he was rudely awoken by the splash of water on his face. Amirzada and Alamzeb were back. This time they had company—Harish Sugandh. Scrawny, and with a salt and pepper stubble, Harish too had his hands tied, and was blindfolded.

'Harish, what the hell are you doing here?'

'I don't know, Mushir bhai. They just picked me up.'

Harish got his own share of slaps and kicks and then faced the same demand for money.

'Amir bhai, the money is all spent. You know how expensive it is to make a movie. The marketing costs even more. And the theatre-wallahs want to be paid upfront for putting up publicity stills. Guarantee money for promoting the movie ...'

The Pathan duo were ruthless mobsters, but they were newbies to the world of business. They bought the story. However, having been on the run from Dawood for some time, they were desperate for cash. They agreed to reduce their immediate demand to two lakh rupees. The remaining twenty-three lakh would have to be paid from the film's proceeds. Mushir had run out of options and realized that he would have to agree to this.

He called Riaz. 'Riaz, please help me. I know our money is all spent. But please mobilize two lakh from somewhere, otherwise they will kill me.'

Riaz cobbled together the sum by the next morning, and the money was handed over. Mushir and Harish were once again tied up, blindfolded, and carried down two flights of stairs. A car drove them for a few minutes and stopped. They untied Mushir and Harish's hands and blindfolds. They were at Carnac Bunder, barely fifty metres from Mushir's house.

Mushir staggered home. Ashamed to show anyone his swollen face and bruised body, he ran indoors and shut himself in his room and did not emerge from it for the next two days. The release of the big movie was only four days away, but he felt there was no way he could show himself to the press, and the world at large in this condition.

Hearing of Mushir's return, Dilip Kumar called several times. But Mushir refused to come to the phone to speak to him. Finally, the actor decided to visit in person and arrived at Mushir's house. Mushir could not dishonour his esteemed guest, so he emerged from his room to meet him.

Dilip sahab was aghast to see Mushir's condition. '*Yeh kya haal bana rakha hai Mushir bhai* (why are you in this state)? Who has done this to you?' he asked, clearly anxious for the producer's well-being.

Mushir narrated what had happened.

'Arre, why are you hiding then? You need to stop these people. I too am a Pathan. These people give a bad name to our community. Call the cops. I will back you,' the veteran star said.

'Who will listen to me, Yusuf bhai? I am influential in Kanpur, thanks to my forefathers. But here, I am a nobody.'

'Don't worry, Mushir bhai. Let me handle this.'

Dilip Kumar went to the phone and called the commissioner of the Mumbai Police, Julio Ribeiro, one of the most reputed people to ever hold the post. He heard the brief story that Dilip Kumar narrated, and said, 'Don't worry. An officer will be with you soon.'

My phone rang. 'Zende, good morning! It's Ribeiro. Come to my office!' he instructed me, and disconnected before I could even say, 'Yes, sir! '

Most police inspectors never get a direct call from the commissioner. I was fortunate to have built a good relationship with Mr Ribeiro over my career. My office was in the same compound of the Crime Branch as the commissioner's, so I was in his office in two minutes.

The security guard ushered me in. As I walked in, I noticed an additional commissioner walking out, looking one part puzzled and two parts upset. His boss had interrupted their meeting to accommodate a meeting with a lowly inspector. That was unacceptable in his eyes.

Mr Ribeiro briefed me about what he knew. He added, 'Look, Zende, I know film producers can be unreliable but if Dilip sahab is involved, the man involved must be respectable. Also, Amirzada and Alamzeb need to be put in their place. We don't need two more brazen dons in this city.'

Immediately after my meeting with the commissioner, I went to Mushir's house. His bruises looked fresh. Ordinary people rarely get hit, and even when they do, it is rarely anything more than a slap or punch. So, when a hardened criminal hits a regular guy, even if he is pulling his punches, the experience is visceral. The pain lingers in the mind, staying there long after the physical pain and scars have faded. Being a policeman, I had seen several people who had suffered such injuries. Mushir was in a bad state. He was visibly shaken and walked with a limp. But I could see that he was seething underneath. He had done no wrong, nothing to deserve this pain and ignominy, and he wanted justice, maybe even revenge.

There was not much he could tell us about his experience, but the one thing that stood out was the boys' chanting from the Quran. His faith had sustained him through the pain. Finding that room was our starting point, but all we had to go on was the chanting he had heard and the picture of the Kaaba on the first floor.

When I shared the incident with my team, one of my team members, Constable Pansare, seemed to recognize the place from its description.

'Saheb,' he said, 'a few years ago, when I was a young policeman at the Azad Maidan Police Station, Amirzada had been arrested for a relatively small crime. I am quite sure that crime was committed in the same room.'

Pansare vaguely remembered the location being in a chawl in Nagpada.

Detection and police work relies on such serendipity. Hard work, detection skills and feet on the ground are all important elements of police work, but sometimes big breakthroughs come from the most insignificant details, and from the junior-most team members who have the presence of mind to keep their eyes and ears open, and are motivated enough to share their insights.

We immediately headed to that location with Mushir. Constable Pansare was spot on. Mushir recognized the room immediately. The place had not even been locked. It was a grey, featureless room with paint peeling off large portions of the walls. There was a subtle odour of bleach and phenyl that failed to mask the underlying stench of stale sweat, and the unmistakable metallic smell of blood. God only knew what vile deeds had been committed there.

Across the corridor was the calendar with the faded image of the Kaaba. Mushir reverentially touched his ears. But the Pathan duo were nowhere to be found. In fact, the neighbours claimed they had been missing since their murder of Dawood Ibrahim's brother, Shabbir.

'Dawood is after them, saab. Where will they hide in Mumbai? They're gone,' I was told.

It was generally assumed that they had fled the city. Any sane person would think so. Dawood had not reached the peak of his notoriety yet, but he was not a man to be crossed, not even among Mumbai's criminal gangs. But the kidnapping was clear proof that the Pathan gang was back in Mumbai, and ready to take on the might of Dawood.

We fanned out across the city to find Amirzada and Alamzeb, and tapped our informant network in the city's criminal gangs. This case involved the producer of a major Bollywood movie that was sure to be written about in every newspaper. It had the attention of the commissioner of the Mumbai Police. And India's biggest movie stars were personally interested in the outcome of the case. Over the years, Dilip saab and I would develop a warm relationship, but even at that time, I knew him to be a thorough gentleman, full of good manners. Everyone, including I, wanted to do right by him.

Our networks ran deep in every bylane and through every petty gang. Gang members passed on reliable, vital tips to avenge some personal vendetta in the gang, or in return for some leniency when it was their turn to be in the law's cross-hairs. In a couple of days, Constable Narayan of our team came to me, and announced,

'Saheb, I have some good news and bad news. What do you want to hear first?'

'I really need to hear some good news. Tell me that first.'

'Ahmedabad, saheb. Amirzada and Alamzeb have both been found.'

'In Ahmedabad? Are you sure? Is the news pucca (confirmed)?' I demanded.

'Not just pucca, saheb, 100 per cent pucca.'

'And the bad news?' I asked.

'They are with Abdul Latif in Kalupur-Dariapur. He is sheltering them.'

'Latif is still active?' I asked. 'Isn't he behind bars under the Maintenance of Internal Security Act (MISA)?'

'*Kai, saheb*. He has five members in the municipal corporation. They got him out of prison in no time. He is out on bail. Latif is the king of Kalupur-Dariapur.'

'True, I am sure he is not happy to see an upstart like Dawood become powerful. No wonder he is sheltering these Pathans. Is Latif a Pathan too?' I wondered.

'*Apne ko kya karne ka, saheb* (What do we do with that, sir)? They are all bastards who need to be behind bars. Please contact Ahmedabad Police for help,' the constable said.

'No, Narayan,' I retorted. 'It's up to us.'

'*Mhanje*? What do you mean, saheb?'

'You have to go there and find them yourself.'

I deputed two officers, Sub-Inspector Jeremiah and Sub-Inspector Bawiskar, to accompany Constable

Narayan. I would guide the team from Mumbai. We would have daily check-ins. There were no cell phones or WhatsApp to keep us permanently connected; we had to make do with what we had, which at that time was a very unreliable landline telephone connection.

Most people, including I, did not have a phone at home. If there was any urgent 'message', a specially designated constable would come home, with a hard-bound, A3-sized, 300-page Message Register. The 'writer' of the police station sending the message would write the message in the designated format in that book. The 'Message Constable' would carry that register to my house. After reading it, I would sign in the appropriate column, and write any relevant action that needed to be taken, or simply, 'Noted'. These Message Registers were stored in the records room of every police station for decades. When you entered the room, you were likely to be greeted by a cloud of dust and yellowed, crumbling paper. You might say the information was stored in the era's version of 'the cloud'.

The man sheltering the Pathans, Abdul Asif Latif, was an interesting character. He would later go on to join hands with Dawood. He was accused of having played a major role in orchestrating the Mumbai blasts of 1993. Ultimately, he fell prey to a policeman's bullet in 1997. But in 1982, he was on his way to earning the title of 'king of Gujarat', at least among his underlings.

In those days, every major criminal had an area he was associated with. It was like his citadel. In Mumbai, Arun

Gawli had Dagdi Chawl, and Dawood had Musafirkhana. In Ahmedabad, Latif had Kalupur; he was its Robin Hood. He had grown from a local goon to being seen as a benefactor of the poor, a local social worker, and later, a politician. Behind all these veils, he remained a hardcore criminal.

Kalupur's history is no less colourful. The first Swaminarayan temple was built there in 1822. To date, the wooden temple is a favourite among devotees. On the other hand, in 1969, the areas near Kalupur had become the site of a big communal riot.[20] Hundreds were killed. It remained a tinderbox of tensions for several years. Even in 1982, a platoon of State Reserve Police was stationed there.

Kalupur would soon see a daring operation being executed by Bawiskar, Jeremiah and Narayan. It was no short of Entebbe for the Mumbai Police; landing in unfamiliar territory and operating under the radar of the local police.

Dressed in plain clothes, they started staking out the lanes of Kalupur. Although it was their first time there, Kalupur was oddly familiar. Every old Indian city with a history of trading has a locality like this. There were very small lanes and bylanes barely enough for a person or a scooter to pass through. Shops ranged from one- or two-people outfits under old stairwells to chaiwallahs to small metal-working and trading places. Unless you were born and raised here, there was no chance you would know your way around the place. But if you were born there, the area took care of you. If you wanted to hide, the lanes would easily swallow you up. Various communities intermingled every day, trading goods, good-natured insults and jokes. Until they didn't. Divided down the centre by Relief Road, once you got into the lanes of Kalupur, there was no let up from the claustrophobic, crisscrossing paths. It was a tinderbox—the kind of place that every Mumbai policeman was used to navigating in Pydhonie, Nagpada, Dharavi, and many others. It was the perfect hideout for Alamzeb and Amirzada. To move around with impunity, and yet be unseen.

The policemen from Mumbai had to maintain a low profile as they looked for the Pathan duo. If anyone realized they were cops, not only would they go underground immediately, there was no telling if our policemen would be safe. The team patrolled the lanes pretending to be civilians, eyes wide open. The problem was everyone seemed to look a little bit suspicious. And anyone who seemed somewhat interesting quickly dissolved into the thick crowds.

At the end of day one, the team was frustrated and tired. They could not really go about asking questions. They had to rely on half-baked information from their Mumbai sources and stake out the supposed safe houses of Latif. They had to blend in, pretending to engage in mundane activities. To avoid suspicion, they could also not stay in one place for too long. We had a short conversation on a scratchy trunk-call line that took a while to connect, but all I could offer them was a few words of encouragement. So, I told them, '*Savadh raha (stay alert)*! Stay focused, stay together and keep a low profile.'

On day two, the team decided to stake out some popular eateries in Kalupur's main square. Pathans are reputed to love a good meal, and there was a good chance of spotting them there. And their hunch was correct. Amirzada and Alamzeb were casually browsing the eateries when Constable Narayan spotted them. Amirzada's picture was in several police stations, and the Mumbai team recognized him the moment they saw him. The problem was, Amirzada also recognized Constable Narayan. He alerted Alamzeb.

'*Bhaag* (run), *Amir*!' Alamzeb shouted, and in a trice, he vanished, lost in the labyrinth of Kalupur.

The team pounced on Amirzada, who was a trifle slower. But he chose the fight response. He raised a huge ruckus. This was his territory. The Pathans 'ruled' Kalupur, and he was damned if he was going to go down without a fight. Always ready for a spat, the lumpen crowd accumulated in no time. Stones were hurled. Soda bottles crashed onto sidewalks from nearby balconies. The team noticed that even Alamzeb was back in the fray. He had recovered his nerve and joined the crowd to fight.

The platoon of the State Reserve Police stationed there swung into action. No shots were fired, but the shrill sounds of the police whistles pushed some of the crowd back, and a few thwacks from the police sticks kept them there. Through the melee, our team held on tight to Amirzada. In fact, not many noticed as they stopped a passing autorickshaw, and bundled Amirzada into it.

'*Bhagao* (rush)!' they commanded.

The hunter was now the hunted. The driver was a doughty fellow and probably emboldened by his *Mission Impossible* Ethan Hunt moment. He did his bit and zoomed into the nearby lanes. There was a small hospital there. In those days, hospitals were among the rare places with a reliable phone connection.

Two of the policemen kept Amirzada pinned down in the autorickshaw while Sub-Inspector Bawiskar ran in and fortunately got through to my desk phone. I had been glued to my desk, waiting for just this call.

'Saheb, what do we do? We have Amirzada. But there is a big mob looking for us. If we go to the police station ...'

'No!' I cut him off. 'No need to involve the local police. Fly down to Mumbai. Right away. Take a taxi to the airport. I will get tickets booked.' Fortunately, we had the backing of the commissioner of police, and we could work the minor miracle of getting plane tickets at short notice.

They did exactly as they were told. In a few hours, they were back in Mumbai. We gave them a swift reception at Santacruz airport. There was no room for celebrations. We had got our man; Amirzada was remanded to the lock-up. But the money was yet to be recovered.

Amirzada turned out to be full of braggadocio. 'Of course, it was I who picked up Mushir. It takes guts to pick up a producer who makes movies with Amitabh and Dilip Kumar. But what will you prove? Where is the money? You will never find it.'

'Two days in jail, and everything will come spilling out of you, Amir,' I snapped.

'Hah, that's what you think! I have seen many jails, and many officers like you.'

Amirzada's arrogance was his undoing though. He cornered a fellow in his jail cell, who was scheduled to be released that day.

'*Jaanta hai main kaun hoon* (Do you know who I am)? Pathan hoon. Mumbai's most feared. Dawood's time is over. We will take over the city again soon. Do you want to do me a favour?'

'S..ss....sure, bhai,' the other prisoner mumbled.

'Take this note,' Amirzada shoved a scrap of paper into his hand. 'Keep it carefully. Take it to the address I tell you. And get my money out. If you do a good job, you will get twenty-five thousand.'

'Ha...an... haan, bhai,' the other prisoner agreed.

This meek fellow had more gumption than he let on though. He had the makings of a good informant. As soon as he was let out, he sought out a constable and told him what had happened. What's more, he handed over the note.

We had our man.

Using that note, we went to Amirzada's Mahim address. We sent a plainclothesman ahead with the note.

Seeing Amirzada's writing, there was no protest, and our man was led to the room with the cash. We followed close behind. It was a criminal's treasure trove—two automatic rifles, seven or eight pistols, and rounds of ammunition. In the 1980s, such weaponry was a rarity in Mumbai. We arrested all his accomplices, including a man called Jaffar.

When he heard the news of the raid, Amirzada broke down and finally explained in detail how the kidnapping had been executed. And then dropped the bomb, 'It was also I who killed Saabir, Dawood's brother!'

Amirzada ultimately paid for this crime with his life. Dawood ensured that. But that is another story.

For us, it was time to celebrate. Amirzada had been arrested. Alamzeb remained on the run for two more years.

Mushir and Riaz were ecstatic when they heard the news that their money had been recovered and the culprit was behind bars. What's more, their mega production, *Shakti*, proved to be a big hit.

When Mushir met me next, he was filled with gratitude.

'Sahab, what can I do for you?' he asked me with genuine sincerity.

'*Mereko kuchh nahin chahiye, humne toh apna kaam kiya hai* (I don't want anything, we have just done our jobs). But if you really feel grateful, please organize a private screening of your film for the policemen who solved your case, along with their families,' I suggested.

'Done, sahab. We will do it next week itself!'

This was a unique celebration. The private movie screening was a first for most officers. Their family members came dressed for the occasion and enjoyed a proper feast of popcorn and cold drinks on the house!

'And that, my dear son,' I said to Nishu, 'is why Mushir feels so grateful that he has sent us the biggest and best dry-fruit box.'

6

THE BRUTAL MURDER OF BABU RESHIM

It was 5 March 1987, 4.15 a.m., at Mumbai's Jacob Circle lock-up.

A man lay dead in a pool of his own blood. He had been shot several times, and his head had been bashed in with a hammer. The man was Babu Reshim, one of Mumbai's most feared criminals, and a close associate of Dawood Ibrahim. He had been in a police remand cell in the heart of central Mumbai, a stone's throw from Agripada police station. Such an incident had never occurred before. I was the inspector in charge of Agripada police station at the time, so it happened under my watch.

It had been less than a year since I had arrested Charles Sobhraj for the second time, and had so much glory bestowed upon me. But now, I was faced with one of the greatest crises in the history of the Mumbai Police.

As it happened, at 3:50 a.m., two black-and-yellow taxis, with registration numbers MRO 737 and MRO 4827, approached the Jacob Circle lock-up from the 'wakda pul' (twisted bridge). They circled around, ensured there were no cops patrolling the outer periphery, and stopped at the main entrance of the two-storey lock-up. Fourteen men, wielding two sophisticated, imported revolvers; two desi, handmade guns; about thirty-four hand-held explosives; and miscellaneous heavy weapons rushed out. They hurled two bombs towards the constable on sentry duty, who was wielding a .303 rifle. The man was horror-struck and panicked, running away to hide behind the sentry box.

The gang marched into the lock-up building, hurling bombs in all directions, churning up a cloud of dust, and setting off a storm of killer ball-bearings that spewed out of the explosives, as they went. There were six more constables in the lock-up area; one of them, Ghate, was at the entrance to the cells. Two gangsters grabbed him by the collar, and demanded the keys that were bulging visibly under his uniform shirt. He resisted. They ripped his uniform and grabbed the keys. The others continued hurling explosives, and now opened fire indiscriminately in the direction of the constables on duty.

All the constables on duty had loaded rifles, and pouches of bullets meant for just such a situation. Yet, not one constable had the courage to fire back. Only one attempted to return fire, but failed. They were all armed yet mute spectators to this spectacle of disgrace and anarchy.

The attackers had a clear target, Babu Reshim. He was in cell number one. Having ascertained that, the attackers threw a bomb at the single tubelight that cast a glow on the area, and immersed it in darkness. Through the smoke and fire of the explosives, Babu had recognized the gang members. One man was clearly in charge—Vijay Utkar—who had been like a brother to Babu.

'Vijya, what are you doing? What's going on?' Babu yelled into the darkness, using Utkar's nickname.

The attackers pulled out their accurate, imported revolvers and responded by pumping him with bullets. The dim bulb in the cell provided enough light to pinpoint his hulking figure. With the smoke all around and explosions echoing around the small space, the report of bullets flying and ricocheting off the stone prison walls was deafening. It was joined by iron clanging on iron. The keys the men had snatched from Ghate had not opened the lock to Babu's cell. Frustrated, the attackers pulled out a hammer, and slammed open the heavy iron lock.

Vijay Utkar entered the cell with two others, hurling abuses at his mentor. Babu Reshim lay motionless, blood flowing out of him in tiny rivulets. He was clearly dead. But Vijay was not done. Babu had escaped too many times. Only a skull-smashing blow of the hammer to Babu's skull satisfied him.

Splattered with Babu's blood and brain tissue, the gang spun around, guns still blazing. A bullet hit Constable Ahire; he later died in the hospital. None of the other policemen could muster the courage to retaliate. The sudden, guerilla-style attack had paralysed them.

At the Agripada police station, not five minutes away, the cops thought there were some firecrackers going off in the area. By the time someone checked, the two taxis with their fourteen occupants had sped away. Six constables and Babu's cellmate, Mithapalli, suffered minor injuries. But the reputation of the Mumbai Police was seriously damaged.

At about 5 a.m., the ringing of my home phone shattered the early morning silence. I could not believe what I heard on that phone call. Dressing in under five minutes, I rushed towards Saat Rasta on my pale blue Bajaj Super scooter.

*

About twenty years ago, as a teenager, Babu Reshim had been a canteen boy at the Mazgaon Docks. Hired as a casual labourer at the mercy of the canteen contractor, he was tasked with running back and forth with trays of tea and snacks. The patrons were dock labourers who did back-breaking work for long hours, under venal supervisors and union leaders. All those who worked there could only rise through life with a lot of smarts and guts. Babu had both. He built clandestine partnerships with the workers, and with their help, stole imported goods awaiting local shipment and sold them to goons. There was a huge market for cut-priced imported electronics in Mumbai and other Indian cities. Business was good, and the connections that Babu built enhanced his stature as 'Bhai'.

Babu lived in the Jagat Smriti complex of buildings in the working-class neighbourhood of Byculla. This was a neighbourhood that housed thousands of workers from the cloth mills that once were the backbone of Mumbai's economy. Workers came chiefly from the Konkan region of Maharashtra, as well as Uttar Pradesh and Bihar. Once settled, they brought in their siblings, who worked in the same mills or worked for a daily wage as head-load porters, painters, masons, vegetable sellers. Ten or even twenty men lived in 100–200 square foot rooms, sleeping in shifts on and below plank beds. They shared a common toilet and bathroom with others on the floor.

These living arrangements were the 'chawls' that had been around since the 1850s, when they were built as a step up from the slums that housed workers.

The chawls were often populated along the lines of the occupants' hometown or religion. The Marathi vegetable vendors (including my own father in the 1930s) lived in the street opposite Byculla station. Muslim weavers from UP and Bihar, called julai workers, congregated around the Julai Ground, a.k.a. Jhula Ground, and lived in the nearby Sakhli Street and Rangari Street areas. This multi-ethnic and multi-religious, testosterone-fuelled community came under the jurisdiction of the Agripada police station. The cloth mills that many of them worked in, like Hindustan Mills, Modern Mill, etc. were also in the same area. Violence and crime, an integral part of the labourers' and mill workers' lives, attracted many as a source of livelihood.

Babu Reshim, Rama Naik and Arun Gawli emerged as the leading gangsters in central Mumbai, and became known as the Byculla Company, or the Rama Gang.

Babu, Rama and Gawli's connection went back several years. Brothers Uma and Rama Naik lived in the Laalvitachi (red-brick) Chawl, not far from Babu Reshim's home in Jagat Smriti building. The impoverished Gawli, evicted by his mother for marrying a Muslim girl, lived with his wife in Dagdi (stone) Chawl, also in Byculla. Gawli was originally the junior member of the gang. In the late 1970s, they were all petty thieves and ran errands for the bigger bosses.

Parasnath Pande ran several illicit 'matka' gambling dens, and also robbed goods being shipped from the Byculla railway yards. Rama's oldest brother Uma Naik was his assistant. But Pande was closer to his fellow UPite, Kundan Dubey. Uma had a relationship with Dubey's sister that the latter disapproved of. In 1978, he found an excuse to ignite a feud between Pande and Uma Naik, and had Uma killed. This angered Rama, and he killed Pande in retaliation. Gawli and Babu had helped him. Pande had close relationships with some policemen, and they made sure his killers were arrested. Rama was also slapped with the dreaded MISA, which meant he was put away for a long time. In prison, he found a godfather and mentor, Varadarajan Mudaliar. 'Vardabhai', as he was called, was from Tamil Nadu, and his life is said to have inspired movies like Mani Ratnam's Kamal Haasan–starrer *Nayakan*. Varda was an astute man and hid his criminal world behind a veneer of social and religious work. He mentored and connected several young criminals, and even built bridges into local politics.

When Rama was released from prison in 1980, he had acquired a fearsome reputation, as well as the guidance and backing of one of Mumbai's foremost gang-leaders.

Another friend of Dubey, Shashi Rasam, the leader of the notorious Cobra gang—whose members were identified by the cobra tattoo on their wrist—attacked Rama after his release, three times over. But Rama escaped unharmed. Rama then sprang an ambush on Rasam, on the Mumbai Central bridge, and hacked him to death. Rama's gang was now the undisputed crime leader in Byculla.

*

In 1982, Mumbai witnessed a defining event in its industrial history. Trade unions led by the powerful Datta Samant, launched a strike that shut cloth mills across the city. Since most of the workers lived and worked in the Byculla area, that area was deeply affected. Tens of thousands stopped work, and mill owners suffered heavy losses.[12] They kept trying to break the strike by any means possible. If they could show that some workers had started back on the job, it would appear as if the strike was broken, and those who did not return would lose their livelihood. Rama Naik smelt a profitable opportunity and aligned with a rival trade union leader, Bhai Bhosale. Some of Rama's goons started impersonating legitimate workers at the factories, while others went about threatening the striking workers to return.

This strike ultimately forced most of the mills to stop operations. Thousands of mill workers lost their livelihood and moved to other areas. But this had two effects. One, acres of mill land in the middle of Mumbai became a ghosttown. Decades later, these have become some of the most prized real estate in Lower Parel. Two, criminal gangs and politicians now formed a strong nexus. This nexus was first formed by Varda through his gigantic Ganpati celebrations in Matunga. The Rama gang brought it to the workers and labourers of Byculla.

During one of Varda's Ganpati celebrations, Rama met Dawood and Bada Rajan, and they forged a bond. Rajan later connected Dawood to David Pardeshi, who avenged Dawood's brother, Saabir's death. David was

---

12 Sumeet Mhaskar, 'How a Strike 40 Years Ago Dismantled Workers' Claim over Mumbai, Hastened its Gentrification', The Wire, 18 January 2022, https://thewire.in/labour/great-textile-strike-mumbai-mill-workers

arrested and moved to a prison in Gujarat. Bada Rajan was also arrested for facilitating Alamzeb's murder. But one of his former gang members, Safalika, dressed as a Customs officer, shot him dead on the steps of the same Sessions Court. Bada Rajan's junior, Rajan Nikhalje, aka Chhota Rajan, took over the gang, and aligned with the Rama gang.

Babu Reshim found an opportunity to strengthen their ties with Dawood. Babu built bridges to the officers in the jail where David was imprisoned. In broad daylight, he drove into the prison premises and drove out with David, straight to Mumbai, where he reunited David with a grateful Dawood. News broke that David had staged a daring escape, using thick ropes to scale the high prison walls.

My first encounter with the gang was a bit unusual. In the Javed murder case (discussed in 'Underworld Menace'), two of the accused, Chor Namya and Narayan, had their pictures appear in newspapers and other media. Since they had become known to their neighbours as criminals, they decided to live closer to others like themselves, and moved to Dagdi Chawl in Byculla, and joined the Rama Naik gang. Extorting protection money from local restaurants and other businesses was a major revenue source for them. The local restaurant union's leader was one Ramanna Shetty, who owned an 'Udupi restaurant' in the area. His nephew, Sridhar Shetty, was a hulking 100-kg bodybuilder who flexed his muscles in the neighbourhood. He got into a fight with another local toughie, Razak. The quarrel escalated, and they decided to get the local strongman, Rama Naik, to resolve the matter. Rama refused to enter their personal squabble and fobbed them off.

Razak then decided to get Arun Gawli on his side. Sridhar heard of Razak's plan and decided to pay Gawli his own visit. He went to Gawli's stronghold in Dagdi Chawl, and asked his henchmen, 'Where is Arun?'

Narayan heard him and was furious. '*Ae*, who are you calling Arun? Say Arun bhai!'

'What "bhai"? He is not any "bhai" to me! Where is he?' Sridhar was uncowed.

'I'll show you who is your "bhai",' Narayan retorted, and pulled out a six-inch brass dagger, which he used to stab Sridhar in his butt.

Shocked at the sight of his own blood gushing forth, the gigantic Sridhar collapsed right there—dead!

Cases were registered against Narayan and Gawli. As leader of the restaurant owners' union, Ramanna Shetty's pride was hurt by the attack on his nephew. In his years in the area, he had seen many goons rise and fall. He decided to seize the opportunity to bring about the downfall of the reigning boss, Rama Naik. Putting a rising crime boss out of action would bolster his own reputation.

Ramanna Shetty pulled some strings, and got the case transferred to the CID, where it came to me. Shetty exerted a lot of pressure to get Rama arrested as the leader of the gang. But there was no case against him, so I refused. It was a stand-off, but there was no evidence against Rama—quite the contrary, since he had already refused to get involved. I said no to entertaining trumped-up charges.

Shetty decided to twist his finger to extract ghee, as the proverb goes. He filed a case in the Bombay High Court against me, claiming we were not arresting Rama for vested reasons. At the same time, he covertly sent me a bribe of two lakh rupees. I spurned his advances, and the high court dismissed his petition.

What went around came around, in due time.

In September 1985, I was transferred as senior police inspector in charge of Agripada police station. The Byculla Company was the biggest nuisance in the area and had been impossible to nab. One of their bases was the Jagat Smriti building complex. It housed mostly honest working folk, along with some of these hardened criminals. These men maintained a vigil for policemen, and whenever one showed up, whoever we were after would take refuge in some innocent man's home, probably at knife-point, and remain untraceable. If needed, they kept moving houses in this fashion, frustrating the policemen's efforts and forcing them to leave empty-handed.

In October 1985, we got a tip-off that about ten people, including Rama, were planning a big dacoity. They had collected knives, axes, swords and even guns for the job. The guns and the gang were all hiding in Jagat Smriti that night.

Our team, including Sub-Inspector Tejale and a few armed constables, waited till they were all likely to have gathered at the meeting place, one of the rooms in the chawl. Then, they stormed the room at midnight. The gang was taken by surprise. Rama was carrying an unlicensed .45 mm revolver, and there were a couple of other local guns. But trained and armed policemen won the day. We arrested them all.

Rama Naik's arrest was a very big deal in Agripada. He had achieved the reputation of being virtually invincible, and someone who was above the law. I believed it was important to win back the faith of the common people in the rule of law and make them feel safe. The next day, we were to take Rama to his home in Laalvitachi Chawl. We wanted to inspect his home for any other weapons or evidence related to his crimes.

I thought this was a good chance to show people that crime does not pay. It is important to not only enforce the rule of law, but also for people to see it being enforced.

The distance from Agripada police station to Lalvitachi Chawl is about a kilometre, and takes about fifteen minutes to walk. All along the route, we made sure the police presence was prominently visible. We posted constables and officers along the route, and walked Rama the entire way in handcuffs. We made sure the people who feared and respected this gang-leader saw him in chains and brought to book by the local policemen. This image of this fake king in his 'domain' needed to be impressed upon the minds of the people.

Word spread quickly, and people thronged along the route to see Rama's humiliation. All the way, Rama walked with his head bowed, and gaze averted from the people he had harassed and lorded over.

Our streak of good luck continued. Later that month, Sub-Inspector Tejale, while riding home on his scooter, spotted another brother, Amar Naik. He chased after him and managed to grab him. Amar was also carrying an unlicenced gun and was booked.

We had arrested two of the big gangsters of Agripada within two months of my moving in as senior inspector. People in the area were starting to feel a renewed faith in law-enforcement. This had another beneficial effect.

Babu Reshim, the other bigwig gangster, was trying to build his career and credentials as a leader among the dock workers. As a former canteen boy, he had observed the workings of the docks, and was able to connect with the pains and problems of the workers. As a local gang-leader, he was able to occasionally use some muscle and solve their problems. His career and reputation seemed to be in a good place, and he did not want them jeopardized. When he heard of Rama and Amar's arrest, he came to meet me.

'Saheb, I have a request,' he said as he stood before me.

'What is it?' I demanded.

'I know I have a crime record. But I am trying to change my ways. Please don't arrest me or make a procession of my arrest,' he beseeched me.

'What do you mean? If you are wanted in any crime, of course, we will come and get you,' I retorted.

'Saheb, whenever you want me, just send a message to me. I will immediately show up, I promise you,' Babu continued in the same tone.

'Okay, I will give you this chance to reform, and rebuild your life,' I assured him.

But old ways and old accomplices are hard to shake off.

Rama was eventually released, and the rising star of the Rama gang made it a magnet for local criminal talent in Byculla. One of their high-potential hires was Vijay Utkar.

Utkar belonged to a traditionally nomadic community of India and Pakistan.[13] They had a settlement in Agripada. He and Babu met in prison, when Babu had been arrested along with Rama for Parasnath Pande's murder. Rama had an ongoing blood feud with a man called Gopi. He did not like that Babu was nurturing Utkar. But Utkar was meticulous and daring and executed big jobs smoothly. Babu loved him, and he rose through the ranks. Babu soon had a big job for Utkar—to kill Samad Khan, at Dawood's request.

---

13 Haroon Khalid, 'The language curse: How proud community names have been reduced to insults in Pakistan', Scroll, 2 October 2016, https://scroll.in/article/817821/the-language-curse-how-proud-community-names-have-been-reduced-to-insults

Samad Khan was the hot-headed nephew of Dawood's arch-rival, Pathan Karim Lala. Samad was the original jail-based mogul. While in prison, he would still run his crime empire, apparently with the cooperation of the jailers. Prison was like a safe haven for him. But once released, he set his sights on getting rid of Dawood. Dawood pre-empted his move and sought Babu to 'hit' him first. Babu gave the 'supari' (contract to kill) to Utkar. One early morning in 1982, as Samad exited his mistress's home in Sikka Nagar, Utkar gunned him down. The mistress was sick of Samad and had leaked his whereabouts.

This was a big job, and the big boss, Dawood, was really pleased with Rama and Babu.

The star of the moment was, of course, Vijay Utkar. Babu took good care of him, paid him a handsome monthly retainer, and gave his family expensive gifts. Rama remained suspicious of this Utkar, but held his tongue.

Utkar was an impetuous hothead, who pushed his limits. One evening, he gambled away the then princely sum of 25,000 rupees that he had collected for Babu. When Utkar could provide no reasonable explanation for his action to Babu, the latter slapped him in front of his boys. Utkar was furious and left for Indore, the base of his community. Here, he met Gopi, Rama's old enemy, again. Gopi and the other men, including Utkar's own father, were not happy that Vijay worked for Babu. They turned him against Babu and promised to fund Babu's murder, probably with the help of Mahesh Dholakia,

Gopi's employer. Mahesh and his brother, Arvind, were smugglers and emerging criminal kingpins in their own right.

A chance to eliminate their bigger rivals—Dawood, Rama and Babu—was just what the Dholakias wanted.

Babu, in particular, was becoming too powerful. He had killed Dholakia's right-hand man, Vijay Mhapankar, at Dawood's instance. Fearing further attacks, some of the smaller gangs, including Dholakia's, approached Chhota Rajan to broker an alliance between them. Rajan was still learning the ropes of leading a gang, and was reluctant. He also suspected that Dholakia was behind Bada Rajan's killing and rejected his overtures. He stayed loyal to Dawood, Rama and Babu.

Babu was also becoming an effective mass-leader. He was able to replace Datta Samant's union in Mazgaon Docks. Intimately familiar with the skunkworks of the docks, he was able to pinpoint the major problems of the dock workers. Corruption was, of course, a big issue, and he started an anti-corruption cell to highlight cases and errant officers. He aligned with another union leader, Bhai Bhosale, and addressed a large public rally. As a mass leader, Babu had taken charge of organizing the Devi festival in the Dagdi Chawl. Local merchants were forced to donate to his goons. I had tried to put a stop to this, but the sums involved were too large and attractive for them to listen to reason. The merchants, fearing for their lives, would not come forward to file a complaint. So, the police could do nothing. Datta Samant's nephew,

Ajeet Samant, tried to use other means to slow down the meteoric rise of Babu Reshim, but nearly paid for it with his own life.

Babu, and by extension, Rama and Dawood, were running away with the Byculla trophy, and his rivals had to find a way to stop him.

Utkar, the man who knew Babu's habits and hideouts intimately, and actually had the guts to fight him, was just the man for the job. Utkar hatched a plot which he could control from Indore.

On the evening of 10 January 1987, Babu was hanging out at a local Byculla restaurant with three of his boys—Mahesh Prabhu, Jabeer and Rajesh, all of whom were Utkar's chosen hitmen. Their friendly banter ran late and became quite boisterous, till Mahesh pulled out a gun and fired at Babu. He missed.

Before Babu could react, Jabeer shot from his desi revolver. It was a low-powered bullet, and it merely burnt Babu's hand. This was enough for the street-fighter, Babu. He picked up the glass bottles at the cash counter, and started hurling them like missiles at his assailants. The attackers were now the targets, and they fled. Babu filed a complaint, but did not name Utkar, who he probably knew was behind the attack. He and his gang went after all the men from Utkar's community they could find.

Over the next seven days, they attacked every man from that community. Their homes in Agripada were burnt down. They picked up one of Utkar's relatives, tortured him, and cut off his ears, in an attempt to find Utkar's whereabouts. In the meanwhile, our team had received a tip-off that Utkar was in Indore.

Utkar, Gopi and the others regrouped to hatch a plan. But Utkar would have to personally do it. Wanted by the Mumbai Police, and being hunted by Babu and Rama's gang, Utkar dared not make a base in Mumbai. He chose Ulhasnagar, which is on the outskirts and was relatively unpoliced.

He put together a gang, and about twelve of them rented three rooms where they hatched their plan. They sourced and stored weapons from their Indore base: thirty-four grenades, three imported revolvers and a couple of desi ones. Their arsenal was ready. Fate delivered Babu to a choice spot, but it was one that would require an insane level of audacity to hit. Perfect for Vijay Utkar.

Raja Kamerkar was a breakaway from Babu and Rama's gang. He now ran his own matka operations. At the Parijat building in Agripada, Kamerkar and his wife were next-door neighbours to Dawood's cousin and her husband, Shekhar Sadankar. The two women routinely squabbled over domestic matters. As a local goon, Raja did his bit to abet the quarrels too. Dawood received news that Raja Kamerkar was harassing his own kin. This would not do. He called Babu and Rama to fix Raja.

On 12 February 1987, at about 3:30 a.m., Raja Kamerkar was loitering outside his house. Babu, Rama and Gawli attacked him with knives, and stabbed him in the butt, as a warning. He was rushed to the hospital, where the police constable on duty, Yunus, registered the complaint. We immediately spread the dragnet to nab the perpetrators. Luckily, we hit pay dirt on day one. Inspector Isapure found Babu in Jagat Smriti building and arrested him. He was remanded to custody till 19 February. The attack and Babu's immediate arrest and seven-day remand became front-page news in Mumbai newspapers. The remand later extended into March. This is just what Utkar needed. He moved towards Mumbai.

The attack was planned for the night of 2 March. Accordingly, Utkar's armed gang—Raju Bhaiyya, Tarachand Khankat, Kishore Murti, Rajesh Decorator, Ravi Bansi and Mahesh Prabhu—reached Sandhurst Road station by local train. They looked for a taxi to take them to the Jacob Circle lock-up, but they could not find one! The plan was cancelled.

They came back on the night of 4 March. This time the taxis were arranged in advance. They picked up Vinod Maria, Jameel Ashfaq, Chandu Sandekar and Rane from Mumbai Central station. Here, they changed into different taxis, split the weapons between themselves, and moved towards their quarry. They had some time to kill and moved around the city for a bit. At Teen Batti, they jettisoned their taxi drivers. They slowly made their way towards a small park in Maulana Shaukat Road, a short distance from the Jacob Circle lock-up. Over tea, they finalized their plans and backup arrangements. One taxi did a drive-by past the lock-up's main gate and learnt that the guard there was dozing. The stage was set. Fate was on their side and Babu Reshim died in the wee hours of 5 March 1987.

*

After Babu Reshim's murder, there was immense pressure on the police to find the attackers. The press, politicians and senior officers were all keen to see and show that Mumbai was not ruled by gangsters. Every day, the media was filled with harsh criticism about how the police were 'inefficient', 'inept' and 'corrupt'. The pressure from all sides was crippling. The state government responded by appointing an independent inquiry commission under Justice Rane.

I was personally attacked in the press for setting up Babu at the behest of Utkar's community. Rama's gang members were foremost among that community, and they insisted to him that I should be made to pay the price. Rama had not forgotten the incident with Ramanna Shetty and told his men, 'Babu was a dear friend of mine. I am keener than any of you to find the people behind his murder. But Zende is not the man. Zende is an honest officer. He will not do such a thing. Even in the past, when he could have put me away for personal gain, he had refused. I don't think he set up Babu.'

Dawood didn't want to accept Rama's view about me. Babu was important to his business, and he wanted revenge for the murder. He tried to implicate me. His business manager, Satish Raje, filed a false affidavit in the Bombay High Court, claiming, 'I had met Babu in prison, and he told me that Zende has kept me in remand under some fake pretext.'

The Justice Rane Commission examined all these statements and affidavits, and absolved me and all other policemen of any involvement in Babu's killing. However, as is typical of these criminal gangs, less than a year later, Rama and Dawood became sworn enemies, and the same Satish Raje was brutally killed in his own bulletproof car by Arun Gawli's gang.

In the face of all the pressure, I kept Sardar Vallabhbhai Patel's famous quote in my heart, 'In all circumstances, a policeman must remain calm.' I knew that media and public opinion is fickle. The same critics would run reams of plaudits the day we arrested the criminals. I had to make sure not to be swayed by the highs or the lows. We had to keep trying. Sometimes luck favours us, and we get quick breakthroughs. At other times, there is failure after failure. Until one sliver of effort bears fruit.

Five days after Babu's killing, three abandoned taxis were found outside Govandi station. One set of clearly identifiable fingerprints was found, belonging to Vinod Maria. We knew that he was part of the gang that killed Babu. In fact, we knew all the attackers—they were well-known criminals, and the guards at the lock-up had identified them all. Besides, Babu himself had been shouting 'Vijya! Vijya!' during the attack. The task ahead was to find the attackers and prove their guilt. This fingerprint was our first thread.

The gang stayed on the run for a long time. From Govandi, they fled to their rented rooms in Ulhasnagar; from there to Karjat; then a train to Chennai. After a week there, they shacked up in a small dormitory in Mangalore. Then, they fled cross-country to Calcutta, to a relative of Maria's. Back then to Nagpur, where they stayed at the dargah of Tajuddin Baba. Finally, they came back to Ulhasnagar.

Now, here's the irony—they had a friend who worked in the central government–owned ammunition factory in Ambarnath, not far from Ulhasnagar. He lived in the staff-quarters there, and was able to rent three rooms for the gang. They were now hiding from the police on government property! This negligence or venality on the part of government officers has been a repeated source of problems for the police in Mumbai. At one stage, even terrorists were housed in the Antop Hill and Matunga government quarters. Officers who were allotted those quarters did not use them, and instead covertly sublet them to unknown people to make some money on the side. Criminals find this a very convenient set-up. Also, since they are government quarters, it is difficult for the police to investigate or raid such houses at short notice. This gives the illegitimate occupants time for getaways.

At the Ambarnath quarters that Utkar and his gang were holed up in, we got a 'full toss' that the local police wasted. One of the residents living next door to the gang complained to the Ulhasnagar police station about the 'suspicious looking gang of seven or eight people' that had recently moved in. After he insisted on some action, the police station sent one constable to enquire. Sending a single man to check on a gang was a serious mistake. Two of the occupants met the constable, and willingly accompanied him to the police station. This gave the others time to escape. The two who went to the police station were also let go after they gave 'satisfactory' answers to the local policemen's questions. The gang that could have been arrested that very day stayed on the run.

However, now, they needed another hiding place. They knew one Lakshmi Waghri, who stayed somewhere in the Brahmanwada area in Ulhasnagar. Her husband, Kanhaiya, was a local goon, and could help them. Late that evening, the gang went to a small bungalow occupied by sometime-accomplices Rodhi and Randhawa. Randhawa was able to locate and call Kanhaiya. They all set off for Kanhaiya and Lakshmi's home to find a safe hideout for the gang. On the way, a quarrel broke out, and the tired and tense gang quickly turned violent. Utkar pulled a gun and shot at Rodhi. Hearing gunshots, some locals rushed to the spot, and thrashed the gang members. Utkar ran away in the melee. Four of the others—Ravi, Gohar, Mhaiskar and Dodi—were badly beaten up and hospitalized. They were arrested, but gave fake names, and refused to say anything consequential. But news of this gun battle, and subsequent arrests reached the Mumbai Police. We knew there were several members of Utkar's family and community in Ulhasnagar, and in collaboration with the CID, we decided to investigate. We recognized the four as part of the gang we were looking for, and had our first success. That boosted our energies.

Utkar criss-crossed the country once again, never staying in one place for long. In the meantime, Rama Naik had confirmed that the Dholakia brothers were behind Babu's assassination. He and Gawli hunted Dholakia down on Pedder Road in downtown Mumbai. Gawli was arrested and remanded to the CID lock-up. Utkar smelled blood again—he decided to hit Gawli in the CID lock-up.

The Jacob Circle attack was audacious enough, but the CID lock-up is in the compound of the Mumbai Police commissioner's office. An attack there would be almost unimaginable, and would be a huge slap in the face for the Mumbai Police. That's just what the audacious Vijay Utkar wanted—to build up his reputation as the unstoppable killer.

He gathered a small gang of three, and started sourcing high-grade weapons—revolvers, bombs and detonators. He acquired enough ammunition to launch a deadly attack on the CID lock-up.

An inspector on my team, Fadnavis, had worked at Agripada earlier, and had a good informant network in the area. He learnt of this attack being planned, and we immediately set our own plans in motion.

he took over the reins of the gang and made Dagdi Chawl his bastion and fiefdom. He built his profile as a popular leader and launched his own political party, becoming an MLA. In 2012, he was sentenced to life imprisonment for murder. He is said to run his criminal operations from the prison. He has reportedly bought out almost all units in Dagdi Chawl, and it is reportedly being replaced by two forty-storey towers in a massive real-estate deal.[14]

*

Although Babu and his killer were both dead, he continued to haunt me for some more time.

In February 1988, I was transferred out of Agripada police station.

Having taken over the Byculla Company, Gawli built up his social profile. Like Varda Mudaliar before him, he used religious festivals as his platform. The Dagdi Chawl Devi Utsav became a huge public celebration, and the immersion of the Devi statue was conducted the day after Dussehra, when the rest of the country immersed the deity. The immersion procession would leave Dagdi

---

14 Vinay Dalvi, 'Once an underworld haven, Dagdi Chawl to make way for shiny skyscrapers', *Hindustan Times*, 27 October 2023, https://www.hindustantimes.com/cities/mumbai-news/once-an-underworld-haven-dagdi-chawl-to-make-way-for-shiny-skyscrapers-101698344584622.html

Chawl at about noon and would finish only by midnight. Thousands of people took part in it.

Along its route, the deity was garlanded by several local leaders. It was recognized as a big celebration of Hindu identity by several groups. Even the Shiv Sena, which had emerged as the main leader of the Hindu community in Mumbai, would applaud this event through the editorials of the Shiv Sena mouthpiece, *Saamnaa*, that party founder Balasaheb Thackeray himself penned. The Sena viewed the immense celebration as a sign that Gawli and the Dagdi Chawl residents were its ardent supporters.

But criminals have no religion and no political affiliation, except to their own selfish gains. What everyone conveniently ignored or forgot was that Gawli funded these celebrations through extortion. Local businessmen would receive a chit with an amount mentioned on it. They were supposed to deliver the money; how they did it was up to them. But if they wanted themselves, their families and their businesses to survive, this was an annual 'insurance premium'. Even Babu had similarly extorted money on a smaller scale. As a Hindu, I was happy to participate in the Devi celebrations, but the extortion pained me. I had tried unsuccessfully to stop it. No one ever filed a police complaint about these extortions, so we could not take any action against the criminals.

In 1990, I took charge as assistant commissioner in the Nagpada Division. Agripada, and its various processions, including Gawli's huge Devi procession, fell in my jurisdiction. As we prepared for the big day, I learnt that the procession would include a gigantic photograph of Babu Reshim, positioning him as a local leader and posthumous patron of the celebration. I put my foot down against this. That the grand procession was funded with extorted money was bad enough, but I would not allow criminals to be eulogized in this fashion. The Dagdi Chawl organizers too dug in, and announced that they would cancel that year's procession owing to this officer who 'favoured Muslims'. They staged a sit-down protest that later turned violent, and we had to lathi-charge them to quell the mob. The next day, the *Saamana* editorial was titled 'Hirwa Zende' (green flag), ostensibly a play on my last name and my 'support for Muslims'.

I felt hurt by this unfounded allegation, but stayed firm. My higher-ups tried to intercede, but I refused to change my instructions. Senior Shiv Sena leaders like Madhukar Sarpotdar visited me and tried to change my mind. I reiterated my position and explained the reason behind it. These organizers were criminals; they had no political or religious loyalties. Babu himself was a close ally of Dawood. We ought not to boost these criminals' efforts and reputations. I even wrote a long letter to Balasaheb Thackeray explaining my point of view. To his credit, he published it prominently in the following day's edition of *Saamana*.

Finally, the organizers and I reached a compromise. The procession would not carry pictures of Babu, but the placards would mention his name. I did not like this solution, but agreed as a mark of respect to my senior officers and the Shiv Sena leaders. Although everything was now agreed, on the day before the procession, the organizers changed their mind. They would now sit in protest through the day and start the procession only in the evening. The promise made to Balasaheb was thus broken.

Shortly thereafter, I took charge as assistant commissioner of the Dharavi Division, which included Balasaheb's home, Matoshree. Later that year, state assembly elections were announced. Instead of supporting the Shiv Sena, as Balasaheb had expected, Dagdi Chawl pulled down all Shiv Sena hoardings and posters in the area, and Gawli launched his own political outfit. Finally, the Sena leadership was convinced about what I had been saying. Madhukar Sarpotdar went out of his way to visit me and acknowledge this on behalf of Balasaheb. *Saamana* too ran an editorial bemoaning the 'divisive Hindutva' of Arun Gawli, calling it a 'landslide in Dagdi Chawl'.

Criminals like Babu Reshim, Arun Gawli, Dawood Ibrahim, and so many more achieve their evil objectives because the people around them or some powerful people support them. The criminals don't have loyalty to either of them—only to their own selfish motives.

Agripada which has been home to criminals for years continues to have high levels of crime.[15] It has caused decades of hardship for the local population. But unless they diligently report crimes and refuse to support criminals in their populist activities, their situation is not likely to improve.

15 Narayan Namboodiri, 'Western and Northern Suburbs of Mumbai lead in Crimes against Women, Kids', *The Times of India*, 16 February 2022, https://timesofindia.indiatimes.com/city/mumbai/western-northern-suburbs-lead-in-crimes-against-women-kids-report/articleshow/89602242.cms

7

UNDERWORLD MENACE: MASTAN TO DAWOOD

'*Bhai ne tohfa bheja hai* (Bhai has sent a gift),' said Lambu Shakeel, proffering a bundle wrapped in newspapers that evidently contained wads of cash.

Shakeel was one of Dawood Ibrahim's henchmen. He had walked into my office in the Crime Branch, next door to Crawford Market (now Mahatma Jyotiba Phule Mandai) in Mumbai.

It was 1982; just a few weeks ago, we had arrested Amirzada in the kidnapping case of the film producer Mushir Alam, and my attention had moved on to other matters.

'What? Why does he want to thank me?' I asked impatiently.

'By arresting Amirzada, you have done Bhai a big favour. He wants to express his gratitude,' Shakeel answered, placing the packet on the table as he talked.

The packet was not tied—it fell open on the table, revealing neatly wrapped bundles of hundred-rupee notes. The amount was at least twenty times my monthly salary.

'I am a policeman. I did my job as a servant of the law and the people, not for Dawood. Pick up your parcel and leave,' I said, returning to the case papers I was working on.

Dawood was the son of Constable Ibrahim Kaskar, and we had seen him growing up in Police Quarters near Lamington Road police station. As a teenager, he ran errands for us. He was comfortable walking around police stations and milling among policemen.

I remembered about two years before this incident with Shakeel, he had casually swung the door to my office open in the same Crime Branch, and stuck his head in. '*Saheb, mi Dawood*,' he had introduced himself in our mutual language, Marathi. Our eyes had met for a brief moment, and I went back to my work. He had got the message and left.

Over the 1970s, Dawood Ibrahim had risen from being an ordinary thief and extortionist to an acknowledged leader among the criminals that ravaged our city.

The old guard of Haji Mastan and Karim Lala, who ran much of the smuggling and organized crime in Mumbai, were arrested under the Conservation of Foreign Exchange and Prevention of Smuggling Act (COFEPOSA) Act in 1974. They were put away for about two years. Soon after, Emergency was declared in India. Personal rights were suspended, surveillance was heightened everywhere, and there was a significant increase in border security. Mastan and Lala, who relied on porous borders for their smuggling business, saw their empires whittle away.

This left the door open for second-tier smugglers, including some of Mastan and Lala's own henchmen, to increase their share of the pie. Mastan and Lala also started to default on their commitments. They all needed muscle to enforce their will and to successfully distribute their smuggled goods and collect monies. Unemployable, frustrated youth took this opportunity to use violence. This group included the brothers Saabir and Dawood Ibrahim, Mohammed Kalya, Saeed Batla, Alamzeb Jangrej Khan, and many others. Some parallel gangs also emerged, such as Amar Naik's gang in Dadar, Rama Naik's gang in Agripada, 'Bada Rajan' Nayar's gang in Trombay, and Philip Pandhare's gang in Bhandup. While they all fought each other, they were also known to opportunistically collaborate, each trying to claim alpha status in this jungle that they were turning Mumbai into. Some public servants across departments were willy-nilly dragged into these battles, and changed the face and reputation of the Mumbai Police forever.

In 1977, one such second-tier smuggler was scheduled to receive a 'Gold Jacket'—a simple belt that had gold biscuits sewn into its lining to avoid detection. At the border, depending on the smuggler's MO, the jackets would be brought in secretly, or a collaborating

Customs officer would seize the jacket, and then hand it over to the smuggler after receiving his own fee. In this particular incident, the Customs officer involved cunningly seized the jacket, and took it home. The smuggler involved was left stumped. His own strength lay in being able to source, land and then distribute this gold. He did not have the muscle or influence to enforce against this truant Customs officer.

Ironically, he chose to come to the police. He tried to file it as a case of theft of his property. But since he did not have a legal right to the jacket in the first place, the police refused to register his case. He was at a loss, and desperate. His livelihood and perhaps his life were at stake here. His customers, many of whom may have paid in advance, would not have forgiven the non-delivery of their goods. Ruthless enforcers would be at his doorstep any minute. Unless, he found one of his own.

It was just the opportunity that an up-and-coming gangster like Dawood Ibrahim needed.

By this time, Dawood had taken to hanging out near the CID office, looking for little opportunities to get 'jobs' helping people whom the police may not be willing or able to help. Dawood gauged the situation of this cornered smuggler and agreed to retrieve his stolen Gold Jacket. The deal was struck for two lakh rupees, about half the value of the jacket.

Dawood called on his old accomplice, Amirzada. In 1973, as up-and-coming criminals, he and Amirzada had together ambushed a businessman, who was driving home near Carnac Bunder in Mumbai. They had robbed him at gunpoint. But they were soon arrested, identified by the victim, and sentenced to five years in jail. That was the only crime that Dawood was ever convicted of.

By 1977, as convicts out on bail, Dawood and Amirzada had started aligning with rival gangs: Dawood with Haji Mastan, and Amirzada and his cousin and partner, Alamzeb, with their fellow Pathan, Karim Lala. But this was a big job, and a reliable accomplice was worth forgetting some rivalries for. Dawood and Amirzada agreed to split the loot fifty-fifty.

Amirzada and Alamzeb picked up the Customs officer and brought him to a small room at Pakhmodia Street, not far from Dawood's own home. They thrashed the man, branded him with hot iron, and tortured him till he confessed, and returned the Gold Jacket. Since the 'client' was Dawood's contact, he collected the promised two lakh rupees but reneged on his commitment to Amirzada. Instead of one lakh, Dawood offered him 15,000 rupees. They could not resolve the dispute, and asked Haji Mastan to arbitrate. He got them to settle at 75,000 rupees. At the rendezvous planned to hand over the money, Dawood attacked them instead. The Pathans were furious and vowed to get their due.

Dawood knew how ruthless Amirzada was and stayed out of his sight. But he kept harrying the Pathans. Amirzada and Alamzeb, on the other hand, waited for an opportune moment to strike back.

Dawood struck first. In July 1977, his friend, Iqbal Natiq, who was the editor of the newspaper *Raazdaar*, wrote an 'exposé' of how the Pathans were operating their criminal businesses in Mumbai. He named Saeed Batla, Ayub Lala, Amirzada and Alamzeb, and provided specific details of their operatives and hideouts. This made them and their operations vulnerable to other gangs, as well as to the police. In fact, the Mumbai Police even began proceedings to have the pair banished (colloquially known as tadipaar) from Mumbai. The Pathans were convinced Dawood was behind this exposé—the details seemed too close to the truth and they guessed that an insider was probably involved.

They extracted a gruesome revenge: they kidnapped Natiq, killed him, hacked his body and threw the pieces into the marshes of Mahim Creek. Amirzada and Alamzeb were arrested for this murder, but they could not be convicted. Their accomplice, Saeed Batla, was convicted and sentenced. The other elder, Karim Lala, then arbitrated a truce between the young Pathans and Dawood. It held ... briefly.

In 1977, Dawood and Amirzada were released on bail. Batla was also released on bail in 1978, much to the chagrin of the Mumbai Police, and to Dawood's delight. He, his brother Saabir, and his accomplice, Khalid Pehelwan attacked Batla, and the truce was broken. They didn't kill Batla, but chopped off his fingers, reciprocating the brutality of Natiq's murder. The Pathan gang were now desperate for revenge, and got their chance in a few months.

Dawood had to go for daily hajiri (attendance) to Nagpada police station, as he was out on bail. He would get checked for weapons, and did not carry any. But, since he had many enemies, Khalid went with him, carrying a concealed revolver.

Amirzada, Alamzeb and their gang were also there in connection with their tadipaar proceedings. They fought a pitched battle right outside the police station. Bottles were hurled, knives and guns were used. Khalid and Alamzeb were arrested, and only later released on bail.

The outlawed Pathans readied themselves for battle. They went to the Chambal area, which in those days was a hotbed of dacoits like Phoolan Devi. They aligned with a notorious dacoit, Mustaqim, and obtained guns, swords and knives from him.

In the meantime, Haji Mastan again arbitrated a truce between the Pathans and Dawood. A wafer-thin peace was restored between the gangs, and unbridled crime against Mumbai's citizens again rose. Khalid committed a robbery with Mohammad Kalya's help, and they became close. However, in another incident, Kalya insulted an elderly woman, Jainabai.

Jainabai held a special place in the crime world—many young gangsters and rising criminals, like Dawood, treated her like their mother. Any affront to her was a personal challenge to these criminals. Kalya was in big trouble. He sought shelter with Amirzada, who obliged. The truce was again broken.

Fate gave the Pathans the opportunity they wanted. On 2 February 1981, while Amirzada, Alamzeb, and their accomplice, Jaffer, were driving past the immensely popular Haji Ali Juice Centre, they saw Saabir, Dawood's brother, enjoying a romantic evening with his mistress, Chitra. They did not notice the Pathans.

Saabir and Chitra soon drove away, tailed by the Pathan gang. Saabir stopped at the Prabhadevi petrol pump. In broad daylight, in front of Chitra, Amirzada gunned down Saabir. Luckily, Chitra hid and escaped with her life.

After killing Saabir, the Pathans possibly figured that unless they killed Dawood immediately, he would come after them. So, they immediately rushed to Dawood's house in Musafirkhana on Pakhmodia Street. There was a gun battle, from which Dawood escaped unhurt. Amirzada, however, took a well-aimed bullet from Khalid's .303 in his leg, and had to flee. Unknown to Dawood, they fled to Gujarat, and hid there with the help of the local Pathan ganglord, Abdul Latif. Dawood kept looking for them high and low.

About a year later, in 1982, they returned to Mumbai, and kidnapped producer Mushir Alam. We arrested Amirzada in Ahmedabad but Alamzeb stayed on the run for a couple of years, until an alert constable had him arrested in Gujarat. He was set to receive bail, but fortunately, we were made aware of his arrest. I was able to get custody of him on behalf of the Mumbai Police.

Amirzada was now standing trial for the dual crimes of Saabir's murder, and the kidnapping of Mushir. He applied for bail, but we needed to keep him in jail.

At the time, I was with the CID, and in charge of both the cases. We had a trump card, Chitra, Saabir's mistress. She had come to the police directly after the killing and given us the details of how Amirzada murdered Saabir in cold blood. However, when it was time to identify Amirzada in court, she panicked at the sight of the burly Pathan gangster and turned hostile witness. We were stuck. Amirzada, one of the most virulent criminals in the city, would be given bail yet again. That prospect was frustrating.

Hope came in the slimmest of forms—the connection between Dawood and Chitra's testimony.

Dawood had identified Amirzada in court as the man who had attacked his house and him. He also specified that Amirzada was wearing blue pants during the attack. Chitra had also testified in court that Saabir's killer was wearing blue pants. Given the circumstances and the history of violence between Dawood and Amirzada, I presented to the court that there was good reason to believe that Saabir was indeed killed by Amirzada, and should not be granted bail. The court agreed with me, and Amirzada was sent back to prison.

That proved to be fateful: for Amirzada himself, and all gang violence in Mumbai.

Dawood, who was still keen on revenge, now knew where to find Amirzada. But organizing a hit in prison would be difficult. So, he went a step further. What he did next shocked Mumbai's police, judiciary and citizens at large.

Amirzada was being tried in the Sessions Court. Things were not going well for us. At the sight of Amirzada, all our witnesses had slowly turned hostile in court.

On that day, the last witness, Dr Khade, who had conducted Saabir's post-mortem, was about to take the stand. Amirzada was in the accused's box, a smirk on his face in anticipation of his imminent acquittal.

Sub-Inspector Isaque Bagwan stepped up to the judge's desk to hand over a report. Amirzada's fearsome reputation, and a phalanx of Mumbai's top lawyers, were about to outdo the Mumbai Police and the lone police prosecutor, Pawar. Bagwan had been working hard for almost a year, preparing our case against Amirzada. However, with every one of the witnesses turning hostile, he was understandably discouraged. I had met him outside just before we both walked in for the day's proceedings and counselled him to stay calm. After all, we had done everything we could have.

Now, as Bagwan was handing over the papers to the judge, a thin, curly-haired man wearing a loose shirt strolled up to Amirzada. Since there were some friends and family seated in the courtroom, the police assumed he was an acquaintance too. Consequently, no one tried to stop him as he walked up to Amirzada. In a flash, the man pulled out a sophisticated .45 revolver and pumped four bullets into Amirzada's chest and head. The Pathan collapsed in a pool of blood right there.

The hired hitman, David Pardeshi, had rehearsed this. He spun and ran towards the open first-floor window. Dawood's men were waiting in a car right below to drive him away.

Chaos erupted in the courtroom. The lawyers and the judge scrambled to take cover below tables or wherever they could. The people who had come to watch the proceedings began screaming in panic. David already had one leg out of the window when he abruptly fell back and collapsed to the floor.

Sub-Inspector Bagwan had shown great presence of mind, kept his calm, and shot David in the leg. David was arrested, but Amirzada had been murdered in a court of law.

Sub-Inspector Bagwan was duly honoured with a President's Police Medal for Gallantry, a very rare honour for a policeman. Bagwan, who went on to win an unprecedented three President's Gallantry Medals, including one during the 26/11 incident, was one of the most unique and special officers in the Mumbai Police. He and I worked closely together for many years, and I am fortunate that he considers me a mentor and guide.

*

I grew up in Pune's Nana Peth locality. Peth in Marathi means a marketplace. As the name suggests, it was an area filled with many shops. There were many wholesalers of grain, and other provisions, and business was good. For some reason, there were also periodic episodes of violence around the house. We were no strangers to scenes of fisticuffs, bottles being hurled, and even some mob violence. My own father was an ustad (teacher) at the local wrestling school. Times were tough, and jobs were hard to find in those days. So, some of the wrestlers became 'strongmen' for local criminals.

When I was about twelve, one such wrestler called Walekar, went rogue. In the evenings, he would get drunk, and walk around with a long, bare dagger in his hand. He would go from shop to shop and extort money. He would threaten passersby, harass the ladies, and generally make a nuisance of himself. Our neighbourhood was suddenly filled with this new dread that threatened even the common folk. This went on for some weeks. My mother forbade me from going out of the house in the evenings.

However, obedience was not my strength.

It bothered me a lot that this lone man with a knife could wield so much power. Even the local policemen, who only carried bamboo sticks, were afraid of the knife-wielding Walekar.

In those days, India's air was heady with the fragrance of newly won independence. We had all participated in the struggle, and mixed with our family's teachings, there was little patience in my heart for such goons like Walekar. I decided to do something about it.

One evening, I was standing on the road, when Walekar set out on his drunken extortion rounds. I was with a couple of friends. It was a cool evening, and I was wearing my usual half-pants (we did not call them shorts in those days) and a shirt. The cool air, and anger upon seeing this thug, made me shiver a bit.

'I am going to stop this guy,' I muttered under my breath.

'What?' my friend blurted in shock. 'What will you do? Don't do anything stupid.'

The other friend chimed in, his voice trembling. 'He is very dangerous. I have heard he has killed several people.'

'I don't even know what I am going to do. But this fellow has to be stopped,' I replied with certainty in my voice and heart.

We saw Walekar walking in the dim evening light. His silhouetted form was swaying, brandishing his notorious dagger. He swaggered into a ghee-seller's shop, not far from where we were standing. We could hear him demanding the proverbial pound of flesh. This was it.

I strode up to him. At nearly six feet, I was taller than most people around me, and quite strong from regular exercise and farm work. I pushed my advantage, and in my loud booming voice commanded, 'Walekar! Drop your knife, and leave right now.'

Walekar turned around and seemed to freeze. No one had talked to him like this before. But he did not yield, or was too stunned to respond—I could not tell in the twilight. I persisted.

'Walekar, are you deaf? I said drop your knife and leave right now. Don't ever come back.'

Behind all the closed windows, the neighbours could surely hear me. The whole area was deathly quiet. There was a loud clang. Of an iron knife hitting the floor. Walekar turned on his heels, crestfallen, head bowed, and left.

I could not believe it, yet I had never felt greater clarity. My heart was thumping with nervous excitement, yet it was swollen with pride. It's like I had found my calling.

I would never bow down to illegitimate power and injustice, and would protect the people around me from those who wielded it. Mahatma Jyotirao Phule (also known as Jyotiba) was an inspiration forBabasaheb Ambedkar, and fought all his life against untouchability in India. His teachings have inspired me too.

Phule said, 'A man who fights injustice against himself is an ordinary man. A man who does not do injustice unto others is a decent man. But a man who fights against injustice done to others is a good man.'

Throughout my life and career, I have aimed to be a good man and refused to be cowed down by any bully, whether a petty criminal or a famous gangster.

It is such life experiences, my own moral and ideological compass and my upbringing that have played an important role in how I have performed my duties as a police officer. I believe all police personnel are responsible for fearlessly getting to the truth, and the root cause of any problem. They need to steer away from political, media and vested interests. That is the only formula for long-term success. In my experience, even jaded people and hardened criminals respect clear thinking, fairness and justice from a policeman, even if it works against them. What's more, they are likely to reciprocate in kind.

Early in my career, I was posted at the Paltan Road police station. Mastan Mirza was an up-and-coming gangster in those days. He had given up his job as a dock worker and used to conduct illicit activities, fronting it all with a hole-in-the-wall bicycle repair shop near the Musafirkhana area in Mumbai.

Mastan enjoyed the political patronage of a minister in the state government, who used the former's street muscle to source and deal in smuggled goods. Although Mastan himself was not yet a smuggler, he amassed enough money to buy himself a used car and had made some venal cop 'friends'. Mastan would provide them the occasional gift in the form of a small luxury, such as a smuggled watch, or lend them his car for special occasions. He had gained quite a reputation in the area.

At some point, he went to Mecca for the Haj pilgrimage and became known as Haji Mastan. I had no interaction with him till then.

Musafirkhana is about half a kilometre from the Paltan Road police station. The area often saw small skirmishes break out between rival petty criminals, or aspiring gangsters. Guns were rare in those days, but knives came out readily enough. This violence was detrimental to local business and traffic, and a source of fear for the common person. We always stationed a constable in the area; his very presence, bolstered by an occasional whack of his cane, ensured that squabbles did not escalate too often. If there were any signs of imminent armed violence, the constable was able to quickly alert the police station for reinforcements.

One day, a newly recruited constable was stationed on duty in Musafirkhana. He was doing his usual rounds when he noticed a Premier Padmini loading what he thought were suspicious-looking packages. He proceeded to ask the driver what those packages were, and that he wanted to inspect them. It was Mastan's car. Mastan walked up to the constable and slapped him hard.

'*Hum kaun hai janta hai* (Do you know who I am)? How dare you question me!' Mastan demanded arrogantly and slapped the constable again.

The aghast and mortified constable feared for his life and ran away from there. This further bolstered Mastan's self-sought 'stature' as the 'king of Musafirkhana'. Not even the state's law enforcers could stop him. The young constable ran all the way to the Paltan Road police station, where he bumped into me. It was obvious something was wrong. He told me of the incident; I was furious. It was bad enough that Mastan was covertly doing what he was, but if he thought he could mistreat a policeman, he needed to be shown his place. No minister or senior officer could protect him from that. I kept calm and worked out a plan.

I recorded a First Information Report (FIR) from the constable who had been slapped. I made sure that the name and description of the assailant were correctly recorded. The procedure done, it was time for action.

I strode over to Mastan's bicycle shop and dragged him out by the scruff of his neck, and with one arm twisted behind him, walked him to the police station. All the goons and his accomplices watched us from the corners of their eyes; none dared to intervene. In my loud, booming voice, I made sure everyone could hear me reprimanding Mastan.

'*Bh**ch***, you think you are a big man? How dare you touch a policeman! I will show you your real stature. Let me see who saves you now,' I thundered.

No one in that lane dared look me in the eye, and I made sure that everyone around could see this 'king' being reprimanded by the State. The State implicitly assures its citizens a safe space to live; the police embody this assurance. In threatening the police, he had threatened the State and its promise of safety. Such threats have to be quelled appropriately. It is every citizen's responsibility and right to do so. Unfortunately, not everyone owns it, and most bow down to these threats. I refuse to.

When I shoved Mastan into the Paltan Road jail cell, some of the other officers were shocked.

'What have you done? He has political protection.'

'That minister will be furious!'

'The deputy commissioner is going to be angry and will tell us to release him.'

My response was clear. 'I don't care who his benefactor is, and who calls for his release. He has committed a grave crime and will be punished.'

And he was too. Mastan was prosecuted for this offence and convicted. Ironically, that was the only conviction he ever received. It had a sobering effect on other up-and-coming gangsters of the area, like Sayeed and Forteen. They understood that there were some lines they could not cross. A notion that became ingrained as much by Mastan's public humiliation as by his conviction.

Mastan too probably never forgot our first meeting. Over the years, our paths crossed a few times. He was always respectful.

It was nearly twenty years later, after I had retired, that I learned exactly how much. My wife Vijaya and I were at a furniture shop in Bandra. A simply dressed, elderly man approached me, and said, '*Salaam, Zende saab*!'

'Hello,' I said, 'but I don't recognize you.'

'It's okay,' he replied, 'you don't know me. I am Abdul. I used to be Haji Mastan's driver.'

'Hello, Abdul. How are you?' I said, wondering why he had approached me.

'God's grace is infinite, saab. I only wanted to tell you a small story. Do you have two minutes?' Abdul continued.

I nodded.

'Saab, many years ago, Mastan bhai would drive everywhere in his Mercedes. There were not many on the roads in those days, and he enjoyed zooming around in his beautiful car. One evening, we were driving near Worli. I stopped at a signal. There was a blue Bajaj Super scooter in front of us. I still remember the number, MAV 2442. Mastan bhai pointed to the policeman who was riding that scooter. He said, "That is Zende saab. Whatever you do, don't overtake his scooter. He deserves our respect." That is the only time Mastan bhai had shown such respect to anyone, especially a policeman. I have waited almost twenty years to tell you this story. Today's chance meeting gave me the opportunity. Thank you for your time, saab. *Khuda haafiz*!'

I felt satisfied that I had done a good job as a policeman—a quiet pride. Nothing like being praised in front of your wife.

*

In 1984, after the assassination of Prime Minister Indira Gandhi, communal violence broke out against the Sikh community. To avoid the violence escalating, we were ordered to put some of the major criminals in preventive custody. Naturally, they did not want to be arrested. One, it was humiliating. Two, it impeded business. Moreover, they worried that once arrested, they would be kept behind bars on one pretext or another.

To avoid such arrests, many of these criminals had even taken on roles as leaders of social organizations, and publicly hobnobbed with powerful politicians and celebrities. This gave them a veneer of respectability as social leaders. In those days, even some celebrities and politicians were not averse to such publicity. Perhaps there were some symbiotic interests.

Anyway, both Haji Mastan and Karim Lala, who were the two main gang-leaders, had to be arrested. The task was assigned to me. A highly unusual task, since no officer had ever arrested them both. It had to be handled with tact and speed.

By this time, Karim Lala, a Pathan peer of Haji Mastan, and leader of the wide network of Pathan criminals, had become the leader of a social organization called Jigar-e-Pakhtoon. It promoted the well-being of the youth in the Pathan community. Mastan, meanwhile, maintained a low profile as a community elder. Both were averse to being put in jail.

I learnt through our network that Mastan was holed up in the flat of his mistress near Cooper Hospital in Juhu. It was a quiet building, and there were no overt signs of Mastan's presence. It was about 4 p.m., and the tree-lined lane was quiet. I got out of the police jeep and told the officer and constables with me to stay back as I went up to the flat alone. I was sure Mastan would cooperate best if we kept this quiet, and I could give him that. No one stopped me from entering the building. I walked up the three floors, two steps at a time, as I always did.

There was no nameplate on the door, but I rang the doorbell. I am pretty impatient at closed doors and always ring the bell in several short bursts. A woman opened the door just a little bit, chain-latch in place. She looked like the woman of the house.

'*Mastan ko bolo arrest warrant hai. Hum lene aaya hai* (There is an arrest warrant for Mastan. I am here to take him),' I told her. No point in beating around the bush.

'There is no one called Mastan here,' she replied, and started to close the door.

A gentle touch from me kept it open.

'Look, I know he is here. Just tell him that Zende is here,' I continued. My voice having no low-volume setting, Mastan probably heard me and came out on his own.

The woman opened the door, and Mastan was standing there, a lean, slightly stooped man, with a grey bushy moustache, wearing a simple lungi and kurta.

'Let's go, Mastan,' I told him.

'*Kya, saab*. I am not well. I cannot go to any jail now,' Mastan protested feebly.

'Mastan, there is an arrest warrant. It is from the top, and probably a matter of national security. It's best if you cooperate.'

He winced.

'Look, I know you don't want to make a big show of this, so I am here alone,' I assured him.

Mastan knew that there was no way he could escape me; I would use force if the need arose, and he knew that. He also knew that I would not arrest him without just cause, and none of his powerful friends would be able to help him. He probably took comfort in the fact that that since I was his arresting officer, he would not be slapped with any trumped-up charges.

'Let's go,' Mastan said, and started walking towards the exit.

We went down the stairs wordlessly, took our respective places in the police jeep—me in the front, and he at the back with the other policemen. We drove to the Remand Cell.

I had one more job that day: arrest Karim Lala. That too passed without incident, giving me the rare honour of arresting two of Mumbai's biggest criminals in one day.

*

In the world of crime fighting, since it is very difficult to put the big criminals behind bars for long, sometimes, there is a strong motivation and even opportunity to take an easy way out—to stick a trumped-up charge on a notorious criminal, and to put them away. There could also be pressure to implicate rivals of powerful public and political figures. For the officer involved, either of these could yield fame and rewards. In today's hyper-visible, high-stakes era, when public memory is very short, one bad headline can ruin lives. In such situations, it becomes doubly important for a cop to stay focused on the task of uncovering the truth and presenting it fully without any bias.

In the 1970s, the Shiv Sena was a rising organization looking for its mass base. They were actively canvassing the local working-class population. This was a niggling challenge to the ruling Congress party. The Sena also threatened the powerful grassroots and trade union organizations of Datta Samant, George Fernandes and other bigwigs. Samant rose to prominence in the 1970s, and post-Emergency, he was described as the man who 'symbolized the mood and struggles of workers most authentically'.[16] Fernandes, who went on to become the Union railway minister in 1989, had made his reputation as the leader of a nationwide Railway Strike in 1974.[17] Rivalries among the various unions ran strong, and occasionally there were violent clashes between their members.

---

16 Sandip Pendse,, 'The Datta Samant Phenomenon—I', *Economic & Political Weekly*, 18 April 1981.

17 'Biography of George Fernandes to hit stands next month', *The Indian Express*, 27 June 2022, https://indianexpress.com/article/books-and-literature/biography-life-and-times-of-george-fernandes-to-hit-stands-next-month-rahul-ramagundam-7993487/

The Bank of India is one of the biggest financial institutions in the country. Its head office on M.G. Road, with its gigantic Doric columns, has long been a symbol of Mumbai's capitalist muscle. Established during colonial times, Bank of India was nationalized in 1969. In 1974, it announced some changes in employment rules that the unions thought were not employee friendly.

The Shiv Sena seized the opportunity and called a massive morcha, protest procession, on 25 March 1974. Thousands of people would march down the arterial D.N. Road and M.G. Road in south Mumbai. There would be impassioned speeches and sloganeering in front of the bank. Tensions were likely to rise. Rival organizations could show up to scupper the morcha, and there would be a thin red line towards violence on the streets.

Such violence was not uncommon in central Mumbai, where many factories and cloth mills were located, and where most of their employees lived in beehive-like chawls.

However, the white-collar environs of Fort and M.G. Road were strangers to such violence. It was a 'posh' and 'safe' area. Being the nation's financial nerve centre, as well as close to the seat of Maharashtra's assembly and secretariat (Vidhan Sabha and Sachivalaya), this area always attracted the highest level of protection.

On the day of the morcha, the entire route from Azad Maidan to Kala Ghoda was closed to traffic. As a precaution, many shopkeepers and hawkers decided to shut shop. Police were deployed at key locations. This route passed by several historic buildings and landmarks like CSMT station, the Times of India Building, and the infamous Phashi Talao (Lake of Gallows) to one side, and Capitol Cinema and the beautiful Empire Building to the other. On the sidewalk, under the Empire Building's outer arches, usually many hawkers sold clothes, cheap electronics, etc. Some of them had shut shop that day to avoid any vandalism or violence from those taking advantage of the morcha.

The morcha started at 2.15 p.m. The day passed off quite peacefully, except for one incident, and a major one at that—outside the Empire Building, one of the hawkers who hadn't shut shop, Javed, was attacked. He was stabbed to death!

The next day's newspaper headlines blamed the Shiv Sena for this incident. They were accused of indiscriminately bringing their violent ways to the city, and endangering vulnerable citizens. All the opposition parties lambasted the government for its ineptitude in managing the 'danger' posed by the rising Shiv Sena. The matter was even raised in the Lok Sabha.

Given the sensitivity of this case, it was handed over to the Crime Branch for investigation. Inspector Jayant Wagle was put in charge, and I was assigned to assist him. Wagle was the first person to win a Police Medal for Meritorious Service, while still a sub-inspector. He was an incredibly talented and hardworking officer. I was lucky to work closely with him. We had capable and resourceful constables like Panwa Shinde and Pandu Jamadar on the team.

The media mounted pressure to get a grip on the Shiv Sena. Since the morcha was being led by the senior Shiv Sena leader Manohar Joshi (who would go on to be chief minister of Maharashtra), they wanted him to be held responsible and arrested. It would have been the easy way out to arrest him and gain some publicity and kudos. It would have been convenient for the political establishment too. But our team was resolved that we were not going to succumb to such media and political pressure. Our job as the police was to find the truth, and that's what we would do.

We started by lining up the basic facts of the case. Javed had been brought to the G.T. Hospital on Lokmanya Tilak Road at 1.35 p.m. on the day of the morcha. He was pronounced dead on arrival, stabbed to death. He had been brought by some hawkers who also had businesses near his.

Based on the Police Control Room records, we knew that the morcha had started from Azad Maidan at 2.15 p.m. How, then, could the people in the morcha have committed the crime? What were we missing? Was this prima facie evidence that someone else had committed the crime? Why? Those questions had to be answered.

We started interviewing the hawkers who had been present on the day of the morcha. They were completely evasive and unsupportive.

Most of the hawkers were non-Marathi. 'Son of the soil' movements in Maharashtra, often led by the Shiv Sena, sometimes hurt their interests. Also, since most of the hawkers operated without a licence, they were routinely evicted or otherwise troubled by the local policemen. That made us their 'enemies' twice over. By not helping us, they were glad to get a small amount of revenge.

Once again, the bridges I had built with them over my years working in the area paid dividends. We also added a carrot—we made it known that the state government was penitent about the damage suffered by the hawkers. They wanted to compensate the hawkers who were present that day and had had their stalls vandalized. The police had been asked to compile such a list. The hawkers now had reason to talk with us, and also to play nice. After that, this is what we learnt.

At about noon, people had seen the assailants—a gang of four to five people—approach and attack Javed. They had come running down the covered walkway outside the Empire Building. Javed did not appear to know the men, who seemed to be randomly ransacking the closed hawker stalls and stealing from them. Javed tried to confront and stop them. There had been an argument, a brief scuffle, and then they stabbed him. They kept running in the same direction as before, towards Azad Maidan. Although none of the other hawkers had the courage to defend Javed, they rushed him to G.T. Hospital when he was stabbed.

We had found the eyewitnesses. Our task was now to find the perpetrators, and evidence of their crime.

Our second clue was that the assailants had not come from the direction of Azad Maidan, where the people were gathering for the morcha. They had come from the opposite direction. We went from hawker to hawker down D.N. Road, to find who was the first person to see them, and where they may have started. This was crucial to determining their identities.

A peanut-seller outside Kitab Mahal provided a crucial clue. The assailants had actually come from the perpendicular Sukhadwala Road, from the direction of Bombay Gymkhana and Cross Maidan. This was a narrow and quiet lane. In view of the Shiv Sena morcha, it was possible that some shops and offices had stayed closed, so the looters had enjoyed a free run. We kept up our inquiries among the streetside vendors and found another clue. The murder was not their first crime of the morning. They had looted a matkawala opposite Excelsior Cinema. Matka is a sort of illegal lottery that was widespread in those days. The winning numbers were drawn from an earthen pot, hence the name. Since his business was illegal, the matkawala had not filed a complaint with the police. But based on our inquiries, we found that he was not the only matkawala robbed on that day—the same gang had robbed one near the VSNL building. Their major haul of the morning, however, had been the big matka operator at Cross Maidan; they robbed him of Rs 5,000.

The first matkawala was happy to receive police help, especially as he could not have asked for it. He provided a really valuable clue—he had been similarly robbed four months earlier too. One of the thieves had been a part of both gangs of assailants. On the previous occasion, the matkawala had filed a looting complaint at the Azad Maidan police station. Matka looters tended to belong to a particular tribe—one of the quirks of the crime universe. If the previous case had been investigated successfully, then our quarry too would be found soon. And they were.

Thanks to the previous case's investigation work, along with some nifty information-gathering by our ace constable, Panwa Shinde, we nabbed the first gang member, Chor Namya. He and his friend had set out to exploit the potential chaos that the morcha might cause to do some old-fashioned thieving. They were joined by three muscled bodybuilders. Once we knew their identities, we picked them up in a midnight raid. They were all booked, and it was clearly demonstrated that the Shiv Sena and its morcha had nothing to do with the murder. I have no political proclivities, but being absolved in this way was a big deal for the Sena. Their leaders Manohar Joshi and Pramod Navalkar personally visited me to express gratitude.

Another person who was grateful was the Byculla Company boss, Rama Naik. Two of the convicts had worked with Rama. But in this case, Rama was not involved in any way. Given the police department's desire to pick up a big fish like Rama, there was pressure on our team to implicate Rama in this murder and have him put away. But I held firm that in this case Rama had no role to play, and we would not falsely implicate him.

Rama and his gang were grateful for this. But that is another story.

8

DHARAVI: THE INCREDIBLE TRANSFORMATION OF ASIA'S LARGEST SLUM

I sat huddled under an umbrella, like every other policeman stationed in Dharavi police station. It was a classic Mumbai monsoon night, with incessant, torrential rain for over twelve hours—and our police station was but a shed with a tin roof that leaked copiously.

Like everywhere else in Dharavi, the lanes around the police station flooded easily, making the premises and police personnel very difficult to access. We had to sit huddled under umbrellas at the few desks that were available to us. There had been incidents where injured, bleeding people came in to report crimes, and the water from the leaking tin roof caused their wounds to get infected, exacerbating their situation.

In general, violent crime usually occurs in the night. Perhaps, lubricated by some alcohol or drugs, people vent out their accumulated frustrations, in the cover of darkness. Therefore, in most parts of Mumbai, police personnel were always available at that time, and in fact, actively patrolled the more crime-prone areas. Prevention is better than cure, after all. Dharavi of 1980 was an exception to this. On my first night duty, I discovered all the policemen huddled up in the shed that was the police station.

'Why aren't you going out to patrol?' I demanded of them.

'Cannot, saheb. It's too dangerous,' one of them mumbled, visibly embarrassed.

'Arre, you are policemen. How can you say it is dangerous?' I shot back.

'Saheb, we understand what you mean. We are not proud at not doing our job. But the entire basti has no lights. If we go out in the dark, the hoodlums beat us up and run away. We have no way to catch them,' the fellow replied.

Dharavi was a horror, located in the heart of Mumbai. Lakhs of people lived there in illegal shanties, built with mud and whatever scrap material was available, like extra-large sheets of plastic stitched together, tin and plastic roofing sheets. The typical Indian ethos of 'jugaad' was reflected in all its splendid glory as necessity became the mother of invention. The shanties were all tightly packed together and built on either side of a network of narrow drains. During Mumbai's intense monsoon rains, the drains ran over, and sewage flowed into people's homes.

There were no toilets or plumbing to speak of; people defecated under the open sky. Unfortunately, it was also the place where people cooked, ate and slept. Running water and electricity in homes mostly came from illegal sources. There were some community taps that were the scene of daily, intense quarrels that sometimes turned violent. Even within these narrow confines, caste and communal lines remained strongly drawn. Most people lived within their own community areas.

The Nadars and Adidravids of Tamil Nadu were two such communities in Dharavi. Large in numbers and dominant in their own trades, their centuries-old caste rivalry culminated in a full-blown riot in 1980. The violent riot raged on for days, and the senior-most police officers came in to pacify them. But to no avail. When the Mumbai Police commissioner, M.S. Kasbekar, arrived, he was greeted with a volley of stones. The great social worker Ahilyatai Rangnekar, who tried to talk peace to the warring clans, was chased away with sickles. Fortunately, the riots remained localized within Dharavi. But they brought attention to this deep social divide, and hence the policing problem in the heart of Mumbai.

In 1661, Portuguese-controlled Bombay was part of the lavish dowry that Princess Catherine of Braganza received during her marriage to the King Charles II of England. The economy of Mumbai grew rapidly under English rule. Fuelled by opium and textile trade, it became a flourishing port. The port, and later, textile mills and other small and large factories attracted traders, mill workers and labourers from across India. Many employees in the organized business of textiles eventually resided in chawls across the city. In the late 1800s, Dharavi became home to the more polluting industries of tanning and leather-making—their workers also made their homes there. The area grew and eventually became home to many less fortunate ones in unorganized and even illegal trades. It eventually earned the ignominious title of 'Asia's largest slum', home to nearly a million people in an area of just 2.4 square kilometres.[18] The area is an extension of the old Dharavi fishing village, towards the mangroves on the edge of the river Mithi, where it flows into the Mahim Bay. While lakhs of people called it home, it was extremely unsanitary and unsafe. People who had nowhere else to live in an ever-growing Mumbai had made this swampland their home. It is now home to several small- and medium-sized businesses and a thriving community, and is sometimes called the 'poor little rich slum'.[19]

During my time there, for many of its occupants, this slum living was still preferable to the penury and starvation that their native villages and towns across India offered. Castes and communities that would not

---

18 'Asia's largest urban slum—Dharavi: A global model for management of COVID-19', ScienceDirect, *Cities*, Vol. 3, April 2021, https://www.sciencedirect.com/science/article/pii/S0264275120314451?via%3Dihub

19 *Poor Little Rich Slum*, Rashmi Bansal, Deepak Gandhi, Westland, 2012

even look eye-to-eye in the hinterland lived cheek-by-jowl here in Dharavi. Some vestigial rivalries and old feuds carried on, though. So, tempers would routinely flare up, and sometimes boiled over into violence.

So, when the aforementioned constable told me it was too dangerous to patrol Dharavi at night, I was not surprised, but quite saddened. This ineffectiveness of the police was surely alienating the public. This was coupled with administrative neglect of the area, which offered only a tin-shed for a police station, and no other civic facilities. Surely, these were the most basic reasons for Dharavi's high crime rate and violence.

Though still a junior inspector, I decided to try and ameliorate the situation in Dharavi.

I brought up this problem with my guru, the great police detective and historian, ACP Arvind Patwardhan. At that time, he was editor of *Dakshata*, the monthly magazine of the Mumbai Police. Mr Patwardhan pointed me to an article about an inspiring police officer from colonial times, Harry Bruin. Lokmanya Bal Gangadhar Tilak wrote a eulogy of Bruin's unique policing methods way back in 1919—he had integrated with the community in Pune and became familiar with several influential and key members of society, so as to leverage their influence for crime prevention and detection. This was a great lesson for me.

I started by addressing the most basic issue of the policemen being seen as cowards. In those days, Eveready used to make powerful torches called

Commander. Powered by four heavy duty 'C' batteries, they were commonly used by security guards and army personnel. I bought ten of them, distributed them among the night patrol policemen, and made sure we always had enough batteries. Now, the policemen could see where they were going, and who was up to what mischief and crime. Enlightened in this fashion, we caught some of the miscreants red-handed, and gave them a good public thrashing before arresting them. The people loved it. They regained some faith in us, and the criminals stopped discounting us as cowards. Above all, our policemen were able to hold their heads high.

Due to the very challenging work and problematic working conditions at Dharavi police station, most policemen would avoid getting posted there. Once posted, they would try their best to get transferred out. While they were still posted there, they would avoid coming in to work. Late arrivals, frequent sick leaves (genuine or malingering), and general apathy towards work were commonplace. Even the senior officers there were very low on energy, and not able to address this issue. This dispirited team could not address one of the greatest policing challenges of our time. So, I decided to inject some team spirit.

I put down 9 a.m. as the designated arrival time for everyone. For every minute's delay, the latecomer had to deposit one rupee in the office kitty. Each month, we would use this collected kitty for an office lunch—some good mutton biryani. Dharavi had some great cooks, and we ordered only from them. This improved timely arrivals at the police station. When the monthly kitty was insufficient to fund the meal, I would pay the difference. Sometimes, I would add some desserts from the famous RTI cake shop in south Mumbai. Policemen had very low salaries in those days, and this meal was quite a treat for most of the staff. This monthly gathering also ensured that the team got some informal time together and built camaraderie. Also, since we ordered from local vendors, we built relationships with them, and they spread the word among their customers that these policemen were alright.

In order to motivate individual policemen, I started the practice of 'Star of the Week'. Each week, we would write up one good thing that a policeman had done the previous week. It was written up in beautiful handwriting on a clean blackboard and displayed prominently outside the police station. This public recognition engendered personal pride among the team, and the desire to do good police work. It also showed the citizens visiting the police station examples of effective policing in their community, and made them familiar with some of the otherwise nameless policemen in the station. It brought us all a little closer. It was the first step in a long journey.

My next focus was to address schisms and issues within Dharavi's communities.

Since most houses in Dharavi were illegal, and almost no government-provided services existed or functioned there, infrastructure was non-existent. Other than the police station, there was one small sub-post office, and that was it. Schools were some distance away; students had to get there on foot. No school transport or taxi wanted to come to Dharavi.

One day, while patrolling the locality in my police jeep, I noticed a few students making their long walk to school. I drove up to them, asked them to get into the jeep, and dropped them to school. They were delighted to get the ride, and the time and energy saved in walking could be used for studies and other activities in school and at home. Parents who saw education as their family's way out of this life were delighted. We made it a practice for the jeep to drop them to school whenever it was not being used for other purposes. We could not accommodate all the children who walked, but this act sent a strong signal to the community.

The Nadars from Tamil Nadu were one of the bigger communities in Dharavi. They wanted to build their own school closer home. They had no funds, though, so they organized daily movie shows. People who would not otherwise donate for the school were happy to buy movie tickets. Policemen would also show up—to collect hafta (weekly tribute). I stopped this hafta collection immediately, and actively supported this unique funding programme. During my patrols, I would make a brief stop there, to make sure things were progressing smoothly. This gave a feeling of security to the people, and audience numbers increased, making fund-raising for the school easier.

Every year in April, the Dalit community would celebrate Babasaheb Ambedkar's birth month by playing movies and songs at a very high volume. This was a common problem across Mumbai—many religious and social occasions were celebrated in this fashion. The celebrations had nothing to do with the occasion itself.

Babasaheb is one of the greatest Indians. He lifted himself out of absolute penury through sheer hard work and a focus on education. His life holds great teachings for us all. Dharavi's Dalits, his ardent followers, however, were clueless about his life and teachings. The community lived in twelve chawl buildings. I bought twelve copies of his biography, written by Dhananjay Keer, and distributed them among the community. During the month of celebrations, I would speak at every major public event, and tell them about Babasaheb's life and teachings. For many, this was a revelation, and inspired them to make their own lives better. I was invited to more, even larger events. The following year, during the ritual garlanding of Babasaheb's statue on his birthday, I was accorded the honour of offering the first garland.

Such outreach programmes gradually reduced communal violence in Dharavi. There was also a steep drop in violent and other crimes, as policemen became more visible, and policing became more effective. We also made Dharavi's people aware of the importance of their own role in stopping crime. The police's powers are limited without public support. We encouraged them to report crimes, and turn in criminals, not harbour them.

We also made them aware of their own right to defend their families and property. Sections 100 and 103 of the Indian Penal Code (now replaced by the Bharatiya Nyaya Sanhita) granted citizens the right to use proportionate force if their being or property was under threat. Under extreme threats of rape or armed violence, citizens could even cause death of the perpetrator without censure.

In a high-crime, highly populated and hard-to-navigate area like Dharavi, awareness of these laws went a long way.

There was one repeat offender in the area who only operated in the dead of night. Before setting out for his night of crime, he would rub black grease all over his body.

Many families and couples in Dharavi slept in the open because their huts were too small or too hot to sleep in. This criminal would slip into the beds of the sleeping residents, hold a knife to the man's throat, proceed to rape the sleeping woman, even rob her of her mangalsutra or other jewellery. He had committed several such crimes, and we were unable to catch him, as no one could identify him.

Thanks to the grease, if anyone caught him during the act, he would literally slip out. The black made him hard to spot in the dark, and impossible to recognize in the daytime.

I encouraged the locals to remember their rights and duties as citizens—stopping crime and criminals is not the sole responsibility of the police.

One woman, who was being attacked in this fashion, shouted out for help. Her neighbours rushed in to help. The man was still in her bed when they set upon him with cricket bats and sticks. The man later succumbed to his injuries. Given the nature of this crime, the outcome was within the boundaries of the law.

In another instance, a young wrestler called Shivaji heard a woman shouting for help near the Matunga railway station. A man had just snatched her gold chain and was trying to get away. Shivaji confronted him. The criminal pulled out a knife, but Shivaji did not back off. Instead, he shouted for help. A few of his fellow wrestlers joined him. Unfazed by the weapon, they thrashed the chain-snatcher, and handed him over to the police. I congratulated them and treated them all to some coconut water.

The surest sign that you are making a positive difference is that existing vested interests begin to oppose you. The Republican Party of India (RPI) was the main political party that relied on the Adidravid community's votes. Some policemen and community leaders who were benefitting from the old ways of doing things incited the local RPI leader, Ramanand Lad, against me. He, in turn, complained to the commissioner, Mr Kasbekar. I was called in.

'What's going on, Zende? Why are you getting involved in politics?' the commissioner demanded.

'Sir, this is the month of Dr Babasaheb Ambedkar's birthday celebrations. He was one of our greatest freedom fighters and nation-builders. But there are many in our city who have not experienced the basic benefits of freedom. I attend these public sessions to make people aware of Babasaheb's life and teachings,' I tried to explain.

'Look, what is the point of getting involved in all these local activities? Why don't you stick to maintaining law and order? You have reduced violence and crime there. That is all we need you to do,' he urged.

'Sir, with due respect, this improvement in the law-and-order situation has only been possible because I have become deeply involved in the community. They believe that the police are improving their lives, and we are. They trust us more, and enable us to maintain law and order,' I pressed home my point.

It took a little longer, but the commissioner saw my point of view, and promised to support me.

*

As in the rest of India, the more volatile tinderbox was the relationship between the Hindu and Muslim communities in Dharavi. Strangely, a common trigger event was funerals. One local Hindu community's funeral processions included drinking, music and dancing. These processions typically passed in front of Dharavi's chief masjid on Dharavi Main Road, and disrupted prayers. On a few occasions, this had caused some skirmishes. So, each time there was a funeral procession, there would be some tension in the area.

Here, neither community was in the wrong. They were only engaging in their own cultural practices. In tightly packed areas where such diverse communities live in overlapping spaces, it is very important for each to respect and accommodate the other. They are like neighbours sharing a space in a building. But this mutual respect can only thrive when community members are on friendly terms with one another. If you are trying to build a relationship with a neighbour, one good way to do it is to visit and wish them on a day when they are celebrating a festival or a major event—preferably with a small gift. The thought matters, not the size of the gift. We were all neighbours here, and I decided to try the same. The forthcoming Eid was a good time to start.

I conferred with the leaders of the Hindu community, and we agreed on the action plan. On the day of Eid, when the Muslims emerged from the mosque after prayers, we met each of them with a rose flower and an 'Eid mubarak!' greeting. The men coming out of the mosque were initially surprised by this—men in uniform wishing them was unusual. But they quickly overcame their scepticism, and saw this act for what it was, a friendly gesture that led to much joy and warmth. Community leaders and members who had so far only met during heated arguments and some formal social events were now engaging in this warm and informal way. Over the years, this has become a common practice in several parts of Mumbai, and play a role in building bridges between people.

The Muslim community reciprocated this gesture. They brought over copious amounts of sweets to the police station just before Diwali. They wanted to distribute them among the local Hindu community. We facilitated that. We later took this programme further and started celebrating national events like Independence Day and Republic Day at the police station. There would be a decorated shamiana, laddoos and samosas from Punjabi Ghasitaram halwai, and cakes from Monginis. There was flag hoisting, followed by small cultural events performed by the local school children. All communities participated enthusiastically.

Such small steps helped to restore peace and build trust among the community. It was a good foundation to build on.

*

In the 1980s, rehousing the slum-dwellers of Dharavi was a major civic agenda. It was a political and social hot-button issue in the city. There were debates between the champions of the slum-dwellers and those who advocated for slum-removal for civic development and beautification. Now, as a part of this community, I sympathized with Dharavi's residents, but also realized that such a slum was not great for Mumbai. We had to at least keep the slum from growing significantly.

One morning in 1981, it was reported that literally overnight, another five to six thousand people had built their shanties over a few acres of the area's swampy mangrove forests. These forests acted as lungs for Mumbai and stopped the flood waters of the river Mithi from flowing into Dharavi. Maintaining them was vital.

We had to evict these new settlers immediately before they settled in. Else, very soon they would strike roots in the space and the community, and it would be very difficult to evict them.

I wrote to my seniors in the Mumbai Police about this problem. But that did not help. The land was owned and managed by the Maharashtra Housing and Area Development Authority (MHADA). So I visited their office, and met the person in charge of demolishing illegal encroachments, Mr Walawalkar.

We, the police, could help remove the newly added shanties, but MHADA would have to take care of the land after that, else they would come right back.

We made a plan, and on the appointed day, the police provided the required security when the MHADA bulldozers came in. It was sad to see these homes being broken, but this was an important duty for me. The residents protested aggressively; there was stone-throwing. I too was hit. But we persisted, and by the end of the day, the slums were demolished, and MHADA took over the land. Shortly, the civic agency proceeded to make it a park that eventually evolved into the Maharashtra

Nature Park. It is a haven for migratory birds and insect life, and popular among local morning walkers.

*

One of the biggest problems the police faced in Dharavi was our own working conditions. The tin-shed we worked out of was cramped and dangerous. Such a police station did nothing to improve the public image of the Mumbai Police, and was actually harming police–public relations. Space and funds to build a regular police station were not forthcoming.

Though there was no dearth of space in Dharavi, most of it had been encroached upon, and was not available for its intended use. For example, roads. The narrow lanes of Dharavi were a major traffic bottleneck, notorious across Mumbai. Thousands of commuters spent frustrating hours negotiating the snail-paced traffic over potholed and unsafe roads. A large tract of land had been identified by the Bombay Municipal Corporation (BMC, now Brihanmumbai Municipal Corporation) for a ninety-foot-wide road. It was cleared out and flattened. However, by the time the government actually started making the road, the land was covered with shanties. As mentioned before, demolishing these shanties was a hot-button issue. Also, it needed extensive collaboration between various government bodies that was hard to orchestrate among divergent priorities.

Due to this, despite various representations by the Mumbai Police to the state government for a new police station, all we had was this shed. The chief minister, A.R. Antulay, had also made reassuring promises, but there had been no action. One such speech by the CM in late 1981 was quoted in a local newspaper. Using this article, I requested a meeting with Kundatai Kadam, the local deputy municipal commissioner. I told her of our plight and requested her help in getting a plot of land on which we could construct a police station.

'Zende, if we collaborate, and do this right, both of our goals can be met. I will get the ninety-foot road going, and you can get a police station,' Mrs Kadam said.

'Certainly, Kundatai. I would be glad to collaborate. What do you have in mind?' I asked, excited about finding a solution.

'You help me clear the road, and keep it cleared till I get the construction going. I will expedite the process at the BMC. And in return, the BMC will not just give you land, but will also build you a police station, at our own cost,' she responded.

'Kundatai, that sounds fantastic, and I will find a way to keep my end of the bargain. But are you sure about the police station being built by the BMC? They are always built by the state government,' I pointed out. I had doubts, because the proposal sounded too good to be true.

'Don't worry, Zende. I will manage that. This road project is really important for the city of Mumbai. And

I am sure building a police station will be a benefit, not a flaw.'

It took a few days. We organized three platoons of the State Reserve Police (about 300 lathi-wielding policemen) to assist us. In fifteen days, we managed to clear shanties over several acres of land in the heart of Mumbai, on the arterial stretch connecting 'town' to the suburbs. Once again, making all these people homeless made us very sad. But the police had a larger civic agenda to support, and this demolition would ease the daily lives of millions of Mumbaikars. Despite vociferous opposition from the locals, we kept our eyes on the task, and got it done.

By May 1982, I had been posted at Dharavi for about two and a half years. What had appeared to be an impossible, Sisyphean task, had turned out to be one of my most satisfying assignments. There had not been any big-name criminals to apprehend, nor many complex, high-profile cases to detect. But serving the people and restoring peace and harmonious relationships among them had been a rare honour for an ordinary policeman like me. There was still a long way to go, and I expected to get about a year more before I would be transferred, as per department policy.

While I was deeply entrenched in matters at Dharavi, larger forces were at play. Julio Ribeiro came in as commissioner of police. Although we had not met, Mr Ribeiro had the reputation of having a bias for action. He was said to understand the importance of police–

public relations. I was excited to be leading Dharavi police station under his guidance, when, quite unexpectedly, I received transfer orders—to the Crime Branch/CID.

I later discovered the reason for this transfer. Reportedly, I had been seen as a loyalist of the outgoing commissioner, Mr Kasbekar. Hence, the transfer to the Crime Branch, whose office was in the commissioner's office compound, where I could be watched closely. I was not happy about the transfer, but took it in my stride.

On my first day, I was asked to visit Mr Ribeiro.

'Mr Zende, I will be keeping an eye on you,' the towering Mr Ribeiro spoke to me in his booming voice.

His presence in that glorious office in the 150-year-old Victorian building, and his punitive tone and words, were all very imposing. But my mind was clear—that I had not done anything wrong.

'Sir, you may have been misinformed. I am only a soldier. It is my duty to follow the orders of my superior officers. You will find that I never flinch from doing my duty,' I replied, respectfully.

'We will see, Mr Zende. I am going to give you a high jump!' he said, and dismissed me.

Back at my desk, I was seething at this treatment. In that moment, I voiced my fury in the choicest words. There were several officers around me, who clearly heard it all. One of them was ACP Madhav Gupte, considered Ribeiro's right-hand man. He spoke up in a firm tone.

'Mr Zende, please mind your language. Don't forget that you have been transferred to the Crime Branch.

After Dharavi, this is like a promotion. If you are indeed such a good police officer, let Mr Ribeiro see it, and you will also see what a good leader he is,' Mr Gupte said.

I was taken aback. What he had said about my transfer was true. In police circles, a posting at the Crime Branch was indeed widely coveted. I publicly vowed to show what a good policeman I was. And true to Mr Gupte's words, I discovered what a fantastic leader, mentor and commissioner, Mumbai Police had just been blessed with.

It took about two years for the new Dharavi police station to be built. It was a well-designed building; the police station was on the ground level. The first floor housed a lock-up, a very useful feature since the Dharavi police station was far away from others, and the area housed several petty criminals that needed to be held in police custody pending judicial procedure. On the second floor, there was a very thoughtfully constructed dormitory for State Reserve Police men. They are often called upon from all over Maharashtra when there is a need for additional hands to perform low-complexity policing tasks, like crowd management. This dormitory made it possible for them to be housed in decent conditions during these assignments away from home.

For the inauguration, the minister of state for home, Shrikant Jichkar was invited. Kundatai Kadam and Commissioner Ribeiro were also on the dais. I had been transferred to the CID by then, and accompanied my senior officer, Joint Commissioner Ramachandran, to the event. As a CID officer, I was dressed in plainclothes, not in uniform. I was seated in the back rows since there were several local leaders and politicians in the front rows. Spanking new buildings were a rarity in Dharavi and a lot of the locals were enthusiastically cheering on. There was a beautifully decorated, large shamiana housing all the attendees, and the vibe was very festive. Speeches were made and dignitaries were garlanded.

At some point, a murmur went up among the crowd. It continued for a while, until finally a local community leader asked for the microphone and announced, 'We are very happy that so many senior dignitaries are present today and have addressed us. But one person who has been hugely responsible for the transformation of Dharavi, including getting us this beautiful police station, is with us, but has not been thanked. Zende saab, please come up on stage.'

I was beaming with pride but smiling sheepishly. I got up from my seat at the back of the audience and walked towards the stage. It took me a moment to notice that the audience had burst into unanimous applause. Some were even standing. I walked quite fast, but this briefest of walks seemed to last forever. The pride I felt reminded me of the Cooperage Ground incident more than ten years ago. This was yet another affirmation that serving people was my greatest motivation, and their love and support was the greatest reward.

When I reached the dais, Mr Jichkar stepped forward, and over the roar of applause, announced, 'We are proud to have such an officer!'

For me, this moment was an alignment of so many wonderful stars. The public, whom I dedicated my life to serve and protect, had rewarded me by acknowledging my work whole-heartedly. My senior officers, who I deeply respected, like Mr Ribeiro, were witnessing that the service they led had capable officers, and as a democratically elected leader, Mr Jichkar was seeing how various public services in his administration could collaborate for the benefit for the masses.

ACKNOWLEDGEMENTS

I want to thank all the people of the Mumbai Police whom I worked with—my seniors, mentors and team members. I am also grateful to the thousands of Mumbai's citizens who taught me and inspired me. They made my career in the police service deeply satisfying.

I want to thank my family and friends, especially my dear wife, Vijaya, for their lifelong love and support.

Finally, I am thankful to Mr Pandharinath Sawant for first penning my memoirs in Marathi; my agent, Smita Khanna Bajaj; and my editor, Trisha Bora, at HarperCollins India.

ABOUT THE AUTHOR

Madhukar Bapurao Zende served in the Mumbai Police from 1959 to 1996. In the course of an illustrious career, he became the first officer to win a Police Medal for Meritorious Service and a President's Medal for Distinguished Service in successive years. He now spends his time between the homes of his three children and in Pune. Hours of exercise, intensely tough sudokus, cooking, and meeting family and friends are his passions. This is his first book.

HarperCollins *Publishers* India

At HarperCollins India, we believe in telling the best stories and finding the widest readership for our books in every format possible. We started publishing in 1992; a great deal has changed since then, but what has remained constant is the passion with which our authors write their books, the love with which readers receive them, and the sheer joy and excitement that we as publishers feel in being a part of the publishing process.

Over the years, we've had the pleasure of publishing some of the finest writing from the subcontinent and around the world, including several award-winning titles and some of the biggest bestsellers in India's publishing history. But nothing has meant more to us than the fact that millions of people have read the books we published, and that somewhere, a book of ours might have made a difference.

As we look to the future, we go back to that one word—a word which has been a driving force for us all these years.

Read.